NEW SAFETY
AND FIRST-AID

By the same authors in Pan Books
NEW ESSENTIAL FIRST-AID

This book has been produced thanks to the help of the Esso Petroleum Company Ltd for which the authors and publisher are very grateful.

NEW SAFETY AND FIRST-AID

A. Ward Gardner, MD, DIH, and
Peter J. Roylance, RD, MB, ChB

Illustrations by Michael Stokes

Pan Books Ltd : London

First published 1970 by Pan Books Ltd,
33 Tothill Street, London, SW1

ISBN 0 330 02598 8

Printed in England by
Sir Joseph Causton and Sons Ltd. London and Eastleigh

Contents

*Bleeding — Wounds — Bandaging —
Unconsciousness — Fits — Fainting — Burns —
Fractures and dislocations — Head injuries —
Wet-cold chilling, its prevention and its
treatment*

Preface

How many of us have stood by at an accident wishing there was something we could do, but aware that our lack of knowledge disqualifies us from helping? First-aid training can enable us to give effective aid to the injured. What may be less obvious is that training can also enable us to foresee and avoid hazards to ourselves and other people both in the home and outside.

I have been aware for some time of the initiatives taken in teaching safety and first-aid in Scandinavian and other European primary schools and I am delighted that Esso can be associated with the publication of a book which will serve both these purposes.

The Medical Commission for Accident Prevention has campaigned for a wider knowledge of these subjects and supports the teaching in this book. It is my sincere hope that *New Safety and First-Aid* will prove to be an important step in saving lives and reducing the number of injuries in this country.

N.P. Biggs
Chairman, Esso Petroleum Company, Limited.

In a Memorandum submitted recently to the Department of Education and Science, the Medical Commission for Accident Prevention had this to say:

'What the Commission has in mind is elementary training for all children from an early age aimed at linking the arts with science and forming a background for further education in behaviour training and study of the humanities. In simple terms to learn (i) how the human body works, (ii) how it reacts to its environment, (iii) how it may be protected from physical, mental and emotional injury, and (iv) how, if it is injured, it may be given the best chances of recovery.'

Acknowledgements

We wish to thank

Chief Fire Officer E.R. Ashill, OBE, MI Fire E
Mr Nigel Gardner
Mr Stephen Goodyear, BEM, BSc(Econ), ARCM
Mr J.L. Hall, MA
Mr Stephen Hargreaves
Dr W.T. Jones, Director-General of the Health
    Education Council Ltd
Dr Eric Jones-Evans
Chief Fire Officer G. Nash, Grad I Fire E
Miss D.R. Parncutt
Mrs Eve Williams

The Medical Commission for Accident Prevention
The Royal Life Saving Society
The Royal Society for the Prevention of Accidents

for help in preparing this book.

Foreword for parents and teachers

This book is written for boys and girls to give them basic information which may be used to preserve their own lives, to save the lives of others and to deal effectively with injuries to themselves or to other people. Road safety is taught in schools mainly from the child-pedestrian viewpoint, but first-aid, together with home, water and cycling safety, do not, at present, generally form part of every school curriculum. There is an obvious need amongst all children for basic instruction in these subjects.

The aims of this book are to show each boy and girl that

1 **Prevention is the best course to follow.**

2 **First-aid,** as self-help (giving first-aid to yourself) or as first-help (giving first-aid to other people) is always a poor second to prevention. However, first-aid can be life saving, can help the work of hospitals, and if properly carried out, can lessen human misery and suffering.

3 **Training is needed before anything happens,** first in order to prevent the events which may result in an injury, and second, in order to act effectively when an injury has occurred.

For the book to fulfill these aims, it must be clear in presentation, easily understood, free from errors, and accurate in matters of fact. For these reasons, the authors would welcome your suggestions for the improvement or amendment of the text and illustrations. Please write to us at:

Pan Books Limited,
33 Tothill Street,
London, S.W.1.

Introduction

The aims of this book are to teach you how to

— PREVENT injuries
— PRESERVE your own life
— SAVE LIVES and PREVENT injuries from getting worse, by the use of first-aid

Prevention is always best. That is why it is listed first.

Every day many people, including children, are injured — at home, on the roads or in other places. Try to imagine how you would get on if you lost a hand, or worse still if you could not walk. Most injuries would have been easily prevented if everyone had acted in ways which are known to be safe. So THINK before you ACT. Make sure that you can continue to get about and enjoy yourself by guarding against injury. A hospital bed is a poor place in which to try to enjoy life, especially when if you had used a little thought you could have avoided being there at all.

The first part of the book tells you about home, water and cycling safety.

The second part is about first-aid.

PART 1

Home safety

Home safety

Water safety

Cycling safety

At home there are many possible dangers which can lead to trouble if they are not seen in time by boys and girls and by their parents. Everyone wants their home to be pleasant, safe and happy, and not a place where they can be badly hurt. But it is only by **prevention** that we can succeed in keeping everyone free of injury and keep the house from being damaged by fire.

Here is a list of some of the commonest dangers which are found around the home

— knives, razor blades and other sharp objects
— electricity
— gas
— medicines
— fires
— hot liquids
— falls
— fireworks
— aerosol containers

We give, on the next page, some ideas about the prevention of each of these hazards.

KNIVES, RAZOR BLADES AND OTHER SHARP OBJECTS

Sharp edges on knives and razor blades make for good cutting — but you have to be sure that the cuts are made on things and not on you or on other people! So, always carry knives shut or sheathed, and keep razor blades in a proper, not a makeshift, holder. In this way, you will not harm yourself or others and will keep a useful sharp cutting edge on the knife.

Never try to catch a falling knife or other sharp tool — let it fall and stand clear. Serious cuts can arise if you grasp or clutch at anything which has sharp edges. Feet and toes too can be injured by sharp objects falling on to them.

There can be many sharp-edged things at home — tins, old bits of metal, and **broken glass.**

Always sweep up broken glass; do not try to pick it up as it will probably cut you. And make sure that you sweep up the lot. A left-over fragment may cause someone else serious injury.

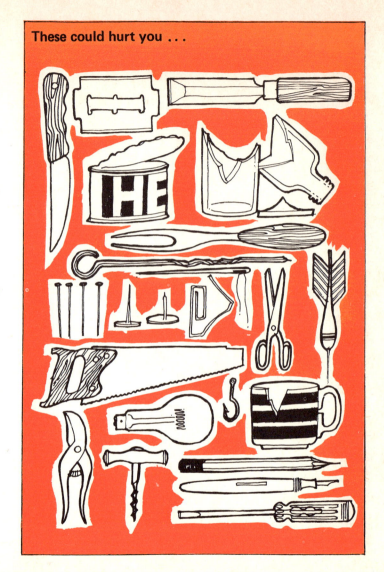

These could hurt you . . .

16

ELECTRICITY

Everyone knows that electricity can be dangerous — both by giving people electric shocks and by causing fires in buildings and houses. But people do not always do the right things with electrical wires and electrical apparatus, and so, some people are hurt, burned and even killed by electricity.

Here are a few do's and don'ts about electricity and electrical apparatus.

— never tamper with wires or take the back off a radio or television set unless you have been taught to repair them properly.

Always switch off before unplugging

OFF
ON
FUSED

— do not cut electrical wires with a knife or pliers unless an adult tells you that it is safe to do so and you **know** that the wire is loose and not connected up at **either** end.

— when plugging or unplugging anything, always begin by turning the electricity **off**. This will prevent you from getting a shock or burn. When unplugging, switch off first and then remove the plug. Similarly, before plugging in, turn off the switch, plug in and then switch on.

— babies and toddlers sometimes try to poke their fingers or toys into electrical sockets — so, make sure that this cannot happen by putting a dummy plug into the socket or by keeping the baby away from sockets. NEVER leave an empty socket switched on. Heavy furniture can be used to stop the baby from getting near and the child can be watched to make sure that he or she does not move into danger.

— because water is a good conductor of electricity, it must never be allowed to come in contact with electrical appliances of any kind in case it gives rise to short circuiting and electric shocks. So, keep water away from all wires, plugs and electric radiators.

— NEVER take an electric fire or radiator into the bathroom — this is always very unsafe. Bathroom-type electric fires should be fitted high on the walls and out of reach, with a special cord switch.

GAS

Make sure that gas fires and gas cookers are completely turned off at the tap after use. Never play with gas cookers, gas ovens or gas fires. Explosions or burns can happen as a result of misuse. A gas cooker may be very hot, and yet not show it.

Lighting gas

1 First light the match

2 Then turn on the gas

3 Light the fire

4 Extinguish the match

MEDICINES

Boys and girls should not take medicines by themselves in case they take the wrong medicine or the wrong amount and thus poison themselves. So, do not take any medicine or pills unless they are given to you be your parents, a doctor or nurse, or by an adult. **NEVER take medicines, tablets or pills unless they are given to you by an adult**

1 Mother reads the label carefully
2 and gives the medicine

Never leave medicines or pills or capsules where toddlers and very young children could find them. The medicines, pills or capsules can be mistaken for sweets with disastrous results. For the same reason, do not eat anything which looks like a sweet unless you are sure that it is a sweet and NOT a medicine. The safest rule is **do not eat anything about which you are doubtful in case it should poison you.**

Keep medicines locked away and out of reach of toddlers

FIRES

All fires — coal, gas and electric — can be dangerous, and must be guarded to prevent people from being burned and setting things on fire. Most burns happen at home — so keep well clear of fires and make sure that the guards are kept in position. Girls, particularly, should be careful that full skirts or nightdresses do not get close enough to a fire to catch alight. Night attire should always be made of fire-resistant materials. Pyjamas or shorties may not look so pretty, but they are much safer than old-fashioned nightdresses. Mirrors should not be put above fireplaces because this may lead to burns by clothing catching fire or by you falling into the fire as you move close to look at yourself. Another frequent cause of burning is reaching for something above a fire or gas stove. Make sure that fires are guarded and that gas stoves are turned off if you have to reach near them. Best of all, do not put things above fireplaces and stoves, and the risk will not then arise.

Portable paraffin heaters should never be moved when alight as this can easily cause fires, and all too often does.

HOT LIQUIDS

Boiling water, soup, tea and many other hot liquids can be spilled and cause a nasty scald if the danger is not foreseen and steps taken to prevent the spill. A teapot near the edge of a table can easily fall or be dragged off. Make sure that toddlers do not grab the edge of a table-cloth and drag a teacupful of hot tea over them or you.

1 *Hot liquids cause nasty scalds*
2 *Don't let this happen*
3 *Pot handles must not be left like this*
4 *This is how (says Indian brave)*

Many two- to three-year-olds — and even some adults — are scalded every day in this way.

On the stove or cooker, see that the pan handles are turned in such a way as to prevent passers-by from knocking the pan off the stove. Make sure also that the handles are not over the flame or heat.

FALLS

It is very easy to fall on a stair or to lean too far out of a window and fall, particularly when standing on a chair which may tip. Try to think ahead and remember the old sailor's motto — one hand for yourself and one for the ship. This means **recognize** the danger, and then act in such a way as to prevent falling. When you use steps, place them firmly and be especially cautious because injuries from falling can easily occur.

Sailor's motto . . .

FIREWORKS

Fireworks are dangerous

Every year some boys and girls are badly injured or burned because of the unsafe use of fireworks, including rockets. Never carry fireworks in your pocket because this can and does lead to serious burns or injuries. Always read the instructions carefully and in a good light. Unless the firework says on it 'may be held in the hand', do not hold and light it. All hand-held fireworks should be pointed away from yourself and other people — especially younger children. Never point a firework at anybody — and remember that the firework hasn't read the instructions and may not behave exactly as you expect!

Every year some boys and girls lose their eyesight as a result of firework injuries — so, make sure that this cannot happen to you. 'Bangers' must not be thrown at people or let off in groups or put under glass jam jars or tin cans. The flying fragments of metal and glass resulting from the explosion can cause very serious injuries.

It is always wise to have an adult present at any firework display.

AEROSOL CONTAINERS

Fly sprays, deodorants, garden sprays, perfumes, hair lotions and many other sprays come in aerosol containers. These containers operate by pressing a button to allow the contents to spray out. The contents are held under pressure in the containers. If such containers are heated, they have no means of allowing the contents to escape as the heat causes expansion of the air or gas inside them, and this leads to greater pressure. The pressure inside the containers rises until a dangerous explosion occurs.

Therefore —

aerosol containers should never be heated, and when empty should not be put on a fire, in an ash-can or heated in any way, in case an explosion occurs.

Many aerosol containers have contents which will burn rapidly, therefore —

aerosols should never be sprayed

— near any naked flame such as an open fire, or a gas ring, or

— near very hot objects such as an electric fire or electric cooker element.

Because aerosols are pressurized they should not be opened with a can opener or pierced by a nail.

FIRE

Every day many fires occur in homes. Nearly all of them are preventable, and are due to people doing things that are known to be dangerous. Numerous lives are lost through fire, and many people, including boys and girls, are severely burned.

An old saying, and a true one, is that 'fire is a good servant but a bad master'. Make sure that you keep fire as a servant.

Never play with matches or meddle with fire-guards; always treat fires and fire-guards with respect.

What to do in case of fire

1 Raise the alarm
2 Send for the fire brigade
3 If the fire is a small one try to put it out if you know how — but take no risks
   If you are unable to put it out quickly, leave the building
4 Check that everyone is safe

Always do these things **in the order given** above. For example, it is foolish to see a small fire, try to put it out and fail, send for the fire brigade and then raise the alarm. If you do not raise the alarm **at once,** this can easily lead to loss of life and may result in a much worse fire and needless loss of life or property.

So, always raise the alarm first and then send for the fire brigade. Next, if the fire is a small one try to put it out if you know how — but take no risks. Lastly, leave the building and check that everyone is safe.

1 **Raise the alarm** so that everyone knows there is a fire and leave the building.

Operate any alarm such as electric bells, a gong, a handbell, or other such warning devices, or shout 'fire' loudly if there is no alarm system.

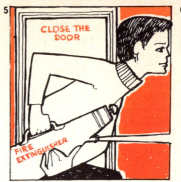

What to do in case of fire
1
2 Raise the alarm by shouting
3 by ringing the fire bell
by setting off the fire alarm
4 Send for the fire brigade
5 Try to put the fire out if the fire is a small one
6 Check that everyone is safe

So far as can be done safely,
— tell everyone in the building that there is a fire.
— wake anyone who is asleep and tell them to leave the building because it is on fire.
— close all doors if you can, especially the door of a room in which there is a fire.
— leave the building quickly unless the fire is a very small one, and help others to do so.

2 **Send for the fire brigade** — so that they can come at the earliest possible moment.
— go to a telephone, read the instructions on the dial and act accordingly — this may say
'Dial 999'
'Dial 0'
or 'Lift receiver and wait for operator to answer'
When the operator answers he will probably say

'Emergency — which service, please, police, fire, or ambulance?' Ask for 'fire' and when connected to the fire brigade, tell them the address to which to send the fire engine and any other help which may be required. Try to give a clear message. If anybody is hurt, ask also for an ambulance.

3 **If the fire is a small one, try to put it out,** but in doing so use care. If the fire is a large one, leave the building.

4 Check that everyone who was in the building is safely out, by having a 'roll call'. If anyone is missing, tell an adult or the fireman AT ONCE, so that a search can be made.

Fire fighting at home

The best thing for putting out fires at home is water. Make sure that at school you know where the fire extinguishers are, and that you know how to make them work **before** there is a fire. Ask your teacher to show you what to do. There are a number of different kinds of fire extinguishers — so learn how to work any extinguisher that is at home or at school or in any other place where you may be. When there is a fire, you will have to act swiftly and surely to put it out!

Some fires need special treatment both to prevent the person attacking the fire from exposing himself to danger and to avoid spreading the fire.

Examples of fires which need special treatment are
— fires in electrical equipment; for example, television sets, refrigerators, electric irons and all wiring, and
— fires in flammable liquids; for example, cooking fats and oils — the 'frying-pan on fire', and fires involving portable paraffin heaters.

Fires in electrical equipment

The most important thing to do is to switch off the current, preferably at a mains switch or at a plug switch and, if possible, pull out the plug. If switching off and pulling out the plug does not put the fire out, water can then be used to put the fire out.

Water must NEVER be used on live electrical equipment. Make sure that the power is off before using water.

Switch off the current and disconnect the plug. Then use water

A 'frying-pan on fire'

Water should **not** be used directly on burning fat or on oils. Cooking-fat fires should be extinguished by smothering. Turn off the heat and cover the pan with a lid or damp cloth. If the liquid has spilled, the same principle of smothering with a damp cloth should prove effective. Never carry a pan of burning fat; you could be severely burned.

Water should be used on the surroundings if the fire spreads. When the fire is extinguished, remove the pan from the heat source and leave it to cool. Keep it smothered until it is cool: do not lift the lid to see if the fire is out in case the fire re-ignites.

1 Switch off
2 Smother with a damp cloth or lid
   DO NOT move the frying-pan
3 Smother spills with a damp cloth
4 Throw water over secondary fires
5 When the fire is extinguished, remove the
   frying-pan from the heat source
6 Leave smothered until cool. DO NOT look
   under the cover. It may re-ignite

Some general hints in case of fire

— always try to stay calm and do not panic; this is easier said than done!

— close the door of the room in which the fire is — this can delay the spread of the fire. Do not open any other doors or windows unless you have to, and if possible shut doors and windows.

— if you are trapped upstairs in a burning building and there is smoke about, try to leave by the staircase. Come down the stairs backwards using your hand on the stair treads as you come down. Keep low and close in to the edge of the stair **next to the wall.** Feel your way down if you cannot see, and lead others with you. Smoke may make you cough and may make your eyes smart, but if you can get out of a fire by going through smoke you should do so. Never turn back unless **heat** or **flame** force you.

1 *In smoke, come downstairs backwards*
  NEXT TO THE WALL
2 *Lead others with you*
3 *If trapped by heat or flame, shut the door*
4 *Put a rolled-up rug or mat at the door*
5 *Attract attention*
6 *Wait to be rescued*

— if you are trapped upstairs by heat or flame and there is no alternative safe way out, shut the door of the room and put a blanket or a mat at the bottom of the door to keep out smoke. Now, wait by the window. DO NOT JUMP or go out of the window, unless you are told by rescuers to do this, or unless the heat is becoming unbearable. Many injuries are caused by panic jumping. In some cases it may be possible to make a rope of sheets and bedding, but this is often rather unsafe and insecurely anchored. By all means make this and have it ready to use if all else fails. But, the best course is to attract attention and

WAIT TO BE RESCUED

Do not jump or use sheets to escape until you are **forced** to do so. Wait for as long as you dare — you will probably be rescued.

If you are trapped only one storey up in any building you may be able to escape quite safely by lowering yourself to arm's length from the bottom of the window and then dropping to the ground. The height of the drop is lessened by your own height plus your arm's length — and this may result in quite a short, safe distance to the ground.

Secondary exits from buildings

Get into the habit of looking for a second way out of any building or room that you are in when you first go to that place. If you already know of another way out, when a fire occurs you are much less likely ever to be trapped.

Clothing on fire

Any person whose clothing catches fire should immediately lie down and roll across the floor. This will prevent the fire spreading rapidly over clothing and will avoid burning the face and inhaling smoke and fumes. If possible, he should roll himself in a rug, keeping his head outside. NEVER remain standing or sitting. If there are other people present, they should grab a coat, blanket or rug and wrap it round him.

The treatment for heat burns is given on p. 70.

Clothing on fire

1–5 Self-help is to lie down and roll. Use a blanket or rug for smothering, if available

6–7 If you see someone on fire, make him lie down and try to wrap him in a blanket, coat or rug

SOME QUESTIONS ON HOME SAFETY

— why are water or dampness and electricity especially dangerous together?

— what may toddlers do if you leave tablets or medicines within their reach?

— why are pyjamas better than old-fashioned night-dresses?

— how should pans be placed on a cooker or stove?

— what are the dangers of aerosol containers?

— are fireworks dangerous? If so, why?

— do you know what to do if there is
1 a fire at school?
2 a fire at home?

— which should you do first, and which next —
send for the fire brigade, raise the alarm, or try to put the fire out?

— how do you come downstairs through smoke?

— what would make you turn back upstairs?

— what would you do in a building on fire if you were in an upstairs room?

— how would you deal with a frying-pan on fire?

— what would you do if someone's clothes caught fire?

— how would you tackle an electrical fire at home?

Water safety

Water can be very enjoyable for playing in, for sailing on, and for swimming in. But water can also be very dangerous for anyone who is unable to swim, or who does not realize the dangers. The sea may look quite safe, but may be dangerous because of strong currents.

Home-made rafts can easily sink, and driftwood used as a boat is unsafe.

Make sure that you come to no harm when you are playing near water by keeping back from the edges so that if you **do** slip, you will not fall in.

Ice melts quickly in the sun, and to be safe to walk or skate on must be of sufficient thickness. So, never venture out on to a frozen pond, lake or river unless an adult tells you that it is safe, and that there is no danger of the ice cracking.

SWIMMING

Swimming provides much healthy exercise and enjoyment, quite apart from its usefulness in preventing drowning. So, try to learn to swim as soon as you can. Many places have swimming baths in which you can bathe all the year round and get expert instruction in the art of swimming.

When you can swim, never go swimming alone or in places where you are not quite sure that it is safe to swim. When swimming, stay near to the shore or bank and keep within your depth, so that you can either put your feet down on the bottom to have a rest, or get out of the water easily. NEVER go out beyond your depth on air rings or air mattresses, and beware of chasing air mattresses or boats out to sea, or into deep water. You can always get another air mattress or boat, but you cannot get another life if you drown in deep water.

Do not go into large waves or surf, even to paddle, unless you have an adult with you.

Patrolled bathing areas — safe and unsafe bathing
In places where there are beach patrols or lifeguards, safe bathing areas will be indicated by red and yellow flags. The patrolled area is between the flags.

Patrolled safe bathing areas will be between two red and yellow flags

Dangerous or unsafe for bathing
A red flag flying indicates that paddling or bathing is dangerous. The danger may be a permanent or temporary one due to weather, tide, or other conditions. If you see a red flag flying, do not enter the water.

Notices in the area should warn you of any permanent danger. These notices will be red, with white letters.

DANGER
DO NOT BATHE WHEN RED FLAGS ARE FLYING

Do not bathe when you see the red flag or where you see a red danger notice

Suitable for surf-board riding. Bathing may be forbidden in such areas

How to rescue a person who has fallen into the water

If someone falls into the water and gets into difficulties, you should try to rescue him; **but you must be very careful that you do not become the next casualty yourself** by falling in. It helps nobody to make two casualties where there was one before, and it makes the work of other rescuers more difficult. Where there is danger for one person in the water, there may also be danger for any other person — you.

The recognized signal to be used by bathers in distress — raise one arm and move it from side to side overhead

It is not always the best action — or necessary — to go into the water to save someone else.
- **reach** out to the casualty by lying down and stretching out a hand, a pole, a branch of a tree or some other handy object.
- **throw** a rope, if handy, to the casualty; or throw some object which will float, such as a large empty can, a beach ball, or a large piece of wood near the casualty. Be careful not to hit the casualty on the head! He will be able to grab the object and to float until you can decide what next to do. A rope attached to a floating object is better than either separately. Try to throw a floating object so that it will be carried by wind and tide towards the casualty.
- **wade** out as far as you safely can — probably not beyond waist level — towards the casualty and then reach towards him using a pole or something else which he can grab and which could pull him to shallow water.

Methods of rescue from the water

1 *Reach out*
2 *Throw a rope*
3 *Wade out*
4 *Throw a floating object*
5 *Row or sail a boat to the casualty. Grab hair*
6 *Jump in and swim to the casualty. You MUST be a good swimmer to be able to tow him back*

— **row** or sail a boat very quickly to the casualty, then grab him by the hair to keep his head out of the water until you can lift him into the boat. Bring him in over the stern: this will prevent a small boat tipping over as it might do if you try to bring a casualty in over the side.

— **swim to the casualty and tow him back** to safety if the above actions are not possible. To do this you **MUST be a good swimmer and trained in life saving.**

Life saving in this way is not discussed in this book because proper and skilled **practical** instruction is required. If you want to learn life saving, ask at your local swimming baths or write to:

The Royal Life Saving Society,
Desborough House,
14 Devonshire Street,
Portland Place,
London, W.1.

An illustrated handbook of life-saving instructions is available from this society which contains full details of how to make a rescue. Practise what the book says in the swimming baths with another good swimmer.

Bring him in over the stern

Having rescued a casualty from the water, you must at once check to see whether he is breathing or not breathing. If the casualty is not breathing, start artificial respiration at once. Every second counts. (see p. 56).

Start artificial respiration at once. Every second counts

If the casualty is breathing but unconscious, place him in the unconscious position with a slight head-down tip and arrange for his removal to hospital (see p. 54).

BOATING AND SAILING

There are two simple rules which will prevent loss of life in most boating and sailing incidents —

1 **Always wear a suitable * well-fitting life jacket when out in a boat.**

2 **Always hang on to, or stay with, an overturned boat,** unless it becomes obviously unsafe to do so — for example, if the boat is approaching a weir or is about to become smashed on to rocks. Even if you are a very strong swimmer, **you must stay with the overturned boat** for as long as you can. A capsized boat is usually much more visible in the water than a person's head, and rescuers will always look first at the boat.

---

* There are many brands and makes of life jacket, not all of which are suitable. However, it is quite easy to recognize those which are suitable — they will have imprinted on them the kite-mark of the British Standards Institution as shown below.

Do not buy a life jacket unless it has the kite-mark on it.

Buoyancy aids are not the same as life jackets. A buoyancy aid is **not** designed to keep an unconscious person afloat face upwards. Buoyancy aids are suitable for conscious swimmers as an aid to staying afloat, but should **not** be confused with life jackets.

— can you swim? If not, when are you going to learn to swim?

— how would you know that bathing was unsafe?

— if somebody fell into the water and had to be rescued, what would you do?

— can you do life saving in the water?

— how would you know if a life jacket is of good design and suitable for the job?

— if you were in a boat which overturned, what would you do?

— what would you do if an air mattress drifted out from the beach into deep water?

— if you were a rescuer in an incident where a sailing dinghy had overturned, where would you look first for the crew of the dinghy?

— what is the difference between a life jacket and a buoyancy aid? Is the difference important — if so, why?

— what does a black and white chequered flag mean when flying at a beach?

— what is the signal to be made by a bather to indicate distress?

Cycling safety

Cycling is great fun and the good cyclist is a help to everyone on the road. To help you to be a good cyclist is the aim of the next section.

BEFORE YOU RIDE

Make sure that your bicycle is in perfect mechanical order and that the riding position is comfortable before setting off. To ensure a safe and pleasurable ride, the saddle should be adjusted for height so that the toes of **both** feet can touch the ground when you stop. In this position, the front parts of the feet will fit nicely on to the pedals. You should not use the instep or heel for pedalling.

The toes of both feet should touch the ground

A comfortable cycling position

The handlebar should also be adjusted for height so that when clasping the handgrips, you lean slightly forward onto them. After making any adjustment to the handlebar or saddle, you should check that they have been securely tightened and cannot loosen under stress.

If any parts of the bicycle are not working properly, you MUST NOT ride. Ask your parents or an adult to check anything which is not working properly.

Make repairs yourself only if you are quite sure that you know the correct way of doing the job. If you are not sure, then you must get advice from your parents, from an adult or from a bicycle repairer. Some cycle shops will carry out a **free safety check** and will advise

young cyclists whether any repairs or maintenance are necessary. Shops where this service is provided display the National Cycling Proficiency window plaque — a red triangle on a circular blue background. Any repairs and maintenance which are subsequently carried out by the cycle shop will, of course, be charged to the owner of the bicycle.

Police officers may visit schools and give cycle safety talks and checks.

The LAW REQUIRES that all bicycles are fitted with:
1 **Two effective braking systems,** one on each wheel. If parents allow children to ride bicycles with ineffective brakes, then these parents can be fined.
2 **A white front light,**
   a red rear light, and
   a red reflector
if the cycle is on the roads during the hours of darkness.

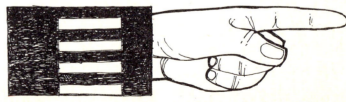

THE LAW REQUIRES

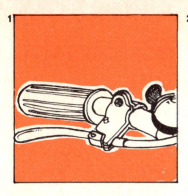
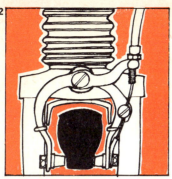

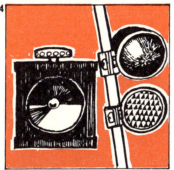

1
2
3 *Two effective braking systems*

4 *A white front light, a red rear light and a red reflector*

5 *One person only may ride a bicycle*

These legal requirements are designed to protect every cyclist — so make sure, in your own interest, that your bicycle is in good mechanical order, that both brakes are efficient, and if you go out after dark that your lights and reflector are working properly.

One person only may ride a bicycle unless the cycle is constructed or specially adapted to take more than one person.

Rear light

If you are buying a battery-operated rear light, ask for one which has the British Standards Institution's kite-mark (p. 32) and BS3648 on it. This will ensure that you get a rear lamp which is well constructed and which will give the best possible light. As your life may depend on having a good rear light when cycling at night, it is wise to buy an approved quality rear light and to see that the batteries are renewed often enough. You should always carry a spare set of batteries in your saddle bag, so that a replacement battery is readily available. Check that the light is working properly when you have put the battery in. It is foolish to risk your life for want of a spare battery!

Before you try to cycle on the roads practise starting and stopping until you can do both without hopping or wobbling. It is not safe to go on the roads until you can control your bicycle properly.

Traffic signs

Be sure that you understand the meaning of traffic signs **before** going on the roads. A pamphlet which shows them all is called 'The New Traffic Signs' (see Appendix).

Two of the most important signs from the cyclists' point of view are given below:

Circular and triangular signs

This sign means STOP AND GIVE WAY to traffic on the major road.

Two continuous white lines are painted on the road beside this sign. You MUST stop at the lines and give way to traffic on the major road, when you see this sign.

If you have to stop because of other traffic before the stop lines, you must stop **again** at the stop lines. Look ahead, then right and left, then right again. Signal clearly if necessary, and enter the major road when it is safe to do so.

This sign means that you must GIVE WAY to traffic on the major road.

At the sign, there will be give-way lines on the road and farther back, a triangle painted on the road, giving warning of the give-way sign ahead. When you reach the give-way lines, you must give way to traffic on the major road.

Before you reach a road junction which has a STOP or a GIVE WAY sign, there may be a warning sign to let you know how far ahead the stop or give-way signs are.

Warning signs

Triangular signs give warning of dangers.

Circular signs give commands and tell you that you MUST or MUST NOT do something.

Balancing

If you have not yet learned how to balance on a bicycle, knot a large scarf round the chest, just under the arms. Mount the bicycle and prepare to pedal. The adult holds the ends of the knotted scarf at the back, steadying just sufficiently to ensure that no spills occur, but lightly enough so that balance can be felt by the rider when going along. By this method, balance can be attained in under half an hour by most learners.

Pedalling

Do not use the instep or heel. Use the forward part of the soles of your feet for pedalling. You will get the best thrust in this way and your foot is less likely to slip.

Braking

The rear brake must always be applied **before** the front brake. NEVER use the front brake alone, otherwise you may go over the handlebar or skid out of control. If you have to stop suddenly and quickly, you can still apply the rear brake a fraction of a second before the front brake. However, if you always ride in an alert way, you should not have to make many emergency stops.

Stopping distance

When you see a hazard and decide to brake, you will still be moving towards the hazard. Several things will determine the length of your stopping distance:

1 how quickly you recognize the hazard and start to apply your brakes. This is called the **'thinking time'**, and may take only a fifth of a second. But, it may also take more than a second, particularly if you are not concentrating. If your speed is 15 mph, you will travel about 4½ feet in a fifth of a second. As your speed increases this **thinking distance** will increase, and as your speed lessens the thinking distance will lessen.

2 the stopping distance will be affected by your **speed.** The faster you travel, the longer will be the distance required by the brakes to stop the bicycle.

3 the **efficiency of your brakes** will determine whether you can stop in a shorter or longer distance. Make sure that your brakes are properly adjusted and that they grip well. When the lever is pulled hard on, the lever should still be a good distance from the handlebars. Badly adjusted brakes can easily lead to brake failure and to spills. **Never** put oil near the brake blocks or on the wheels rims where the brakes grip.

4 in **wet conditions,** the tyres will not grip the road surface and the brake blocks will tend to slip more easily on the wheel rim — so, braking will be less good in wet conditions.

Therefore, when you ride, remember that your stopping distance is made up of thinking distance, plus braking distance, and adjust your speed so that you have time to think and brake before encountering any hazard.

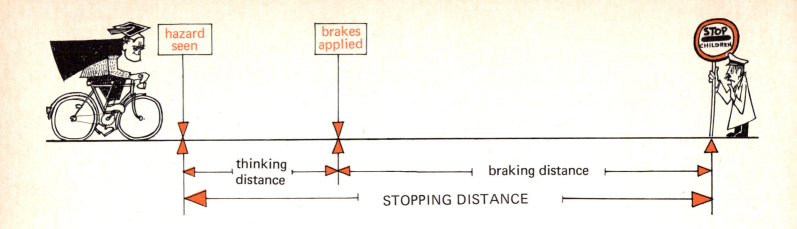

hazard seen

brakes applied

thinking distance

braking distance

STOPPING DISTANCE

Stopping distance is made SHORTER by	Stopping distance is made LONGER by
alertness — early recognition of hazard and short thinking time	**non-attention** — hazards not recognized soon enough, and thinking time longer
slow speeds	**fast speeds**
well adjusted brakes	**badly adjusted brakes**
dry road surfaces	**wet** road surfaces
dry, non-greasy wheel rims and brake blocks	**oil or grease on the wheel rim or brake blocks**

CYCLING ON THE ROAD

If a cycle track is available alongside the road, always use the cycle track.

On the road, cyclists should not travel more than two abreast, and if traffic is heavy or the road is narrow, single file is much safer. Try not to wobble out into the road in case a vehicle is near you.

Never cycle closely behind any car, bus or lorry — their brakes can usually stop them much more quickly than yours can — so you may easily run into the back of them if you are too close, even though you may be able to cycle faster.

Do not hang on to a car or lorry to get a tow. It is a very dangerous practice and is, therefore, illegal.

When in heavy traffic, do not weave through stopped traffic or squeeze in between vehicles which are at a standstill. Riding up the inside of a line of stopped traffic is dangerous. The drivers of the vehicles may not see you, and when they start to move you may be trapped and sustain severe injuries. Good cyclists never weave.

If you stop behind large vehicles, such as buses, vans or lorries, try to stop well behind them and slightly to the left, so that the driver can see you in his near-side mirror. The driver will then be able to make allowance for your being there when he starts moving. However, never assume that he has seen you — keep out of his way and do not move into risky spots.

Gears

If your bicycle has gears, always use a low gear for starting. If you are approaching a hazard and have to slow down, change into a lower gear **before** you reach the hazard. By doing this, you will be ready to move off again without having to change gear while in the hazard area.

For example, when you approach a crossroads and know you have to slow down, change from high to normal gear as you approach. If all is clear and you do not have to reduce speed, you are in the right gear to cycle on past the hazard.

If, on the other hand, you have to slow down further or stop, you should engage low gear so that when it is safe to go, you can pedal easily at slow speeds.

1 Starting from the kerb

2 Starting in traffic

3 Stopping in traffic

Starting

Engage low gear, and before starting always look behind you to see what other traffic is on the road. Wait until any vehicles which are close behind have passed you and look again to see if it is safe to proceed. Signal 'I am moving out' and join the traffic stream.

In traffic

— starting

When you start change to low gear, and with one foot on the ground and the other on a pedal in the up position, be ready to move off.

— stopping

When you have to stop in traffic, keep a good distance between you and the vehicle in front.

— cycling

Stay in line. Do not weave through stopped traffic. Cycle at the left side of the road, close, but not too close, to the kerb. Allow other traffic to pass you whenever possible.

1 Approaching a pedestrian crossing with people crossing

2 Starting from the crossing

3 Look behind you and signal before stopping

Pedestrian crossings

If there are people crossing or waiting to cross as you approach, signal 'I am slowing down and stopping'. Then, stop at the crossing, close into the kerb. Allow the people to cross, then prepare to start again — low gear, foot on pedal in the up position. When everyone has crossed, start gently and move out slightly from the kerb without swerving.

Stopping

Look behind you, then signal 'I am slowing down and stopping'. Move slowly over towards the kerb and stop gently. Change to low gear ready to start if you are going off again.

Never stop suddenly or without signalling except in emergency.

Road junctions and crossroads

A good cyclist will always take extra care on approaching a road junction or a crossroads. A silly cyclist can be hurt and can cause damage to others who may suddenly have to avoid him or her. Remember that not everyone on the roads is a skilled or sensible driver, and that they may not be concentrating fully.

There will often be more traffic, much of which is coming and going in several directions. When you approach a road junction or crossroads and wish to go straight on, or wish to turn left or right, you must know how to do these things correctly and safely. The following diagrams show you how to do these things properly, so that you are not a danger to yourself or other road users.

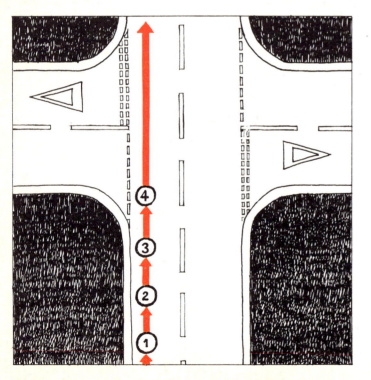

Going STRAIGHT ON on a MAJOR ROAD

4 Look right and left, then right again. If clear, increase speed and clear the crossing.
3 Look out for traffic which overtakes you and may turn left in front of you.
2 Watch for traffic coming towards you which may turn in front of you to enter the road on your left.
1 Recognize hazard of crossroads ahead. Slow down so that you can easily stop at the junction.

Giving signals when cycling

Signals are given to tell other road users what you intend to do. To be useful, the signals must be given
— clearly
— correctly, and
— in good time.
Make sure that you help other road users by giving useful signals.
Do not tell them what to do!

A note about carrying things on a bicycle

In order to control a bicycle properly, **both** hands must be available for steering and braking. It, therefore, follows that school satchels, parcels, hockey sticks and other things should **not** be carried in the hand.

A proper carrier (bag) must be used and if hockey sticks have to be carried, special clasp fittings should be used.

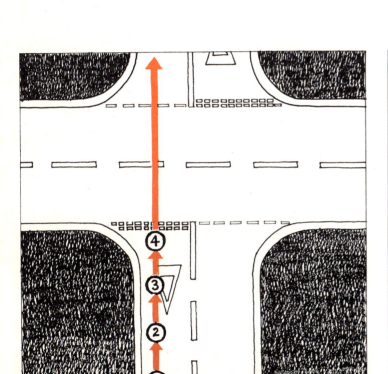

Going STRAIGHT ON on a MINOR ROAD

4 Stop at the line if there is traffic on the major road. Look right and left, then right again. If clear, move quickly across the major road to clear crossing.
3 Look out for traffic which overtakes you and may turn left in front of you.
2 Give-way warning on road and give-way lines ahead. Be ready to stop at the give-way lines if required. Watch for traffic coming towards you which may turn in front of you to enter the road on your left.
1 Recognize the hazard of crossroads ahead. Slow down so that you can easily stop at the junction.

Cycling in the dark — a warning and some hints

Extra special care is needed when cycling in the dark, because the cyclist cannot be seen so clearly by other road users.

Here are a few hints for safer cycling in the dark:

— make sure that the lighting on the bicycle is in good working order. Absence of a good rear light at night makes cycling **extremely dangerous** (see pp. 35, 46), so DO NOT ride your bike at night in the absence of a good rear light.

— always wear something reflective or white, or wear light-coloured clothing so that you can be seen easily in the dark. Plastic reflective material (eg Scotchlite) can be taped to carrier bags or to clothing. This will help to give other road users a clear indication of your presence and may also make your cycle look more stylish.

— take special care when turning right at night. DO NOT turn right at night in the same way as you do by day (see p. 46).

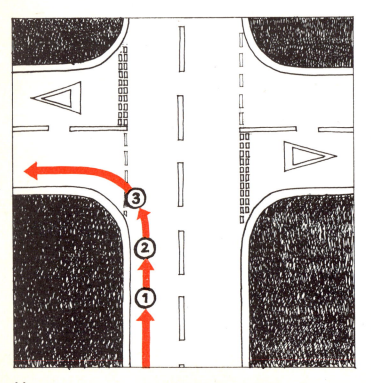

Turning LEFT

3 Check that no traffic is coming from your right and that no traffic is turning from ahead of you into the left-hand road, then turn left and stay close to the kerb.

2 Slow down for the crossroads. Change into normal or low gear.

1 Give the signal for a left turn in plenty of time. Keep close to the kerb all the way.

— when pulling out — for example on starting or to avoid obstacles — be especially careful at night. Motorists cannot see you so easily and may not expect you to pull out.

CHECKING THE SAFETY OF BICYCLES —

a footnote for parents and adults

There is a constant need to check the safety of bicycles which are ridden by children who are under the age of sixteen. In law, parents are responsible (see p. 34) for certain safety requirements such as efficient brakes and lights. However, the most important reason for constant checking must be the safety of the child. Example and concern by parents and adults will instil correct attitudes in children about the importance of safety in this and in other fields. It is folly to allow children to ride unsafe bikes.

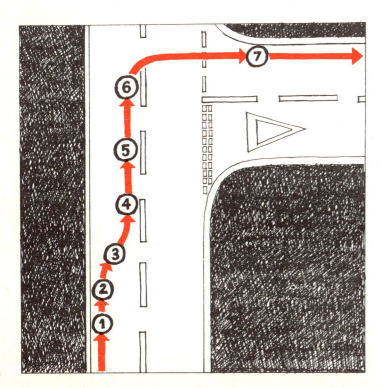

Turning RIGHT in DAYLIGHT

7 Take up position close to nearside kerb. Watch for pedestrians on the crossing.
6 Look ahead, then right, left and right again. Check for crossing traffic and again for approaching traffic. When the way is clear, turn right.
5 Slow down, change into normal or low gear, and, if necessary, stop to allow approaching traffic to clear the crossing.
4 Signal again for right turn.
3 Move into outer lane when near the turning but not too soon.
2 When traffic permits, signal your intention of moving out in preparation for a right turn.
1 Look behind and check on following traffic.

A GOOD CYCLIST WILL

— always give signals clearly and in plenty of time so that other road users know what he or she is going to do.
— keep his or her bicycle in good mechanical order, and will take special care of the brakes and lighting.
— be alert at all times when on the roads.
— know and obey the highway code.

A GOOD CYCLIST WILL NOT

— cycle with a parcel hanging loosely over the handlebar or with an insecure load on the carrier or rear mud-guard.
— have a duffel bag held by one hand over the shoulder, leaving only one hand to control the bicycle.
— ride two abreast on narrow roads.
— make sudden alterations in course.
— alter course without first giving a clear signal.

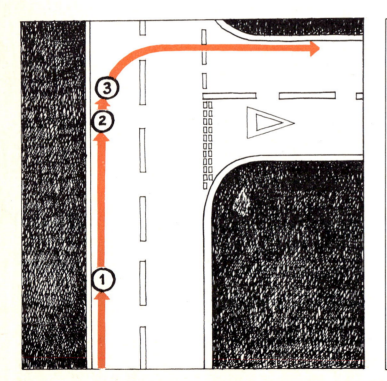

Turning RIGHT at NIGHT

3 Wait for the crossing to become free of all traffic, signal your intention to turn right and move rapidly across, keeping near to the kerb on the new road.

2 Slow down and **stop** at the crossing, **close to the kerb** where you can see the lights of traffic near the junction. Change into low gear, one foot on the kerb and the other on the pedal in the up position, ready to move off.
At night, with dynamo lighting, if you stop your lights go out. So, you must NOT stop in the middle of the road in making a right turn at night.

1 Cycle close to the kerb. Do **not** get into the outer lane.

Make sure that you are a good cyclist. Try also to think what all the other road users are or may be going to do. In this way, you can anticipate their actions and keep out of trouble yourself.

SOME QUESTIONS ON CYCLING SAFETY

— if you were asked to ride a strange bike, what would you check before setting off on it?

— what must by law be fitted on all bicycles?

— how many people are allowed on a bike?

— do you know the road signs and the road lines for 'stop and give way' and for 'give way'?

— what do circular road signs mean?

— what do triangular road signs mean?

— how do you apply the brakes correctly on a bicycle?

— what is meant by the stopping distance?

— what do you understand by thinking distance and braking distance?

— what makes the stopping distance shorter?

— do you know the signal for 'I am slowing down and stopping'?

— do you know what is meant by 'weaving' in traffic? Is it a safe or unsafe thing to do?

— what differences are there in turning right on a bicycle by day and by night?

— can you list three things that a good cyclist will do?

— can you list four things that a good cyclist will not do?

A FINAL NOTE ABOUT PREVENTING INJURIES

Before leaving this section devoted to safety, and going on to read about first-aid, it is as well to remind yourself that you are neither immortal nor invulnerable. At any moment you may find yourself in danger of serious injury, sometimes through no fault of your own. You may also cause injury to others, without any intention of doing so, or without being hurt yourself.

Nearly all injuries are avoidable and most are very easily prevented. Common-sense, courtesy and consideration for others, plus a knowledge of the hazards of any activity can help you to reduce injuries both to other people and to yourself. On the other hand, foolish and impetuous behaviour can only lead to misery. So,

THINK before you **ACT.**

PART 2

First-aid

First-aid and Home treatment

It is always best to prevent injuries, but if injuries have occurred, good first-aid can save lives and prevent suffering. If you know how to do first-aid, you may be able to save your own life and the lives of others, and will know how to treat injuries correctly.

First-aid is of two main kinds, self-help and first-help.

Self-help

Self-help is what you can do **for yourself** if you are injured.

First-help is what you can do for **other people** if they are injured.

Self-help and first-help together are first-aid.

The aims of first-aid are to

— save lives.
— treat injuries so that they will improve or not become worse.
— relieve pain and suffering.
— send the casualty to hospital or to a doctor for further treatment.

The first aim, to save lives, is by far the most important. If you can get a live casualty to hospital, then much can be done for the casualty by the doctors and nurses in hospital. However, nothing can be done for a dead casualty.

Home treatment of minor injuries is **not** first-aid as we have defined it. In home treatment of minor injuries you hope to carry out **all** the treatment which is required without having to send the casualty to hospital or to a doctor. Home treatment could be described as 'only-help'.

WHAT TO DO IN FIRST-AID

Do what has to be done in the **correct order** and **then get the casualty to hospital** or to a doctor without delay. If serious injuries are present, do not try to treat any trivial injuries because the casualty will not die of these; they are not immediately dangerous. But he may easily die from the serious injuries if you waste time. Therefore, send the casualty swiftly to hospital after you have done what is **essential** in order to **save the life** of the casualty. In carrying out first-aid, the order of doing things is very important. For example, if somebody has stopped breathing and has a small cut on his finger, we must first deal with the problem of 'not breathing' because he may die very quickly if he does not breathe. He will not die from a small cut on his finger. Therefore, the treatment for not breathing must have **priority** over the treatment for a small cut on the finger. We can work out the priorities for dealing with any other situation in a similar way.

Below you will find a synopsis of priorities.

PRIORITIES — the correct order of doing things

1 **Look after yourself** — do not become the next casualty.
2 If necessary, remove the casualty from a **position of danger.**
3 Check that the casualty is **breathing.** If not, treat for blocked breathing and apply artificial respiration, by mouth-to-nose or mouth-to-mouth method (pp. 56-7).
4 Stop any **severe bleeding** by pressing where the blood comes from (pp. 60-1).
5 If the casualty is breathing but **unconscious,** turn him into the unconscious position (pp. 54-5). The order of doing 2, 3, 4, 5 above will depend on what exactly has happened. But in any particular case, it should be obvious which is the urgent problem.
6 Cover all bad wounds and serious burns (pp. 86-7).
7 Prevent movements of any parts of the body which you think may have a fracture (a broken bone) (p. 75). Do the same if the bone ends are dislocated (out of joint) (p. 80).
8 If serious injuries are present, get the casualty quickly to hospital. Do not delay the arrival of a seriously injured casualty at hospital by attempting to treat trivial injuries or any other condition which does not threaten life. The priorities of 2, 3, 4 and 5 may vary, but in any particular case the correct order should be obvious.

Always send for help

If there are more than a very few minor casualties or if there are any seriously injured casualties, **sending for help must have a very high priority.** In most cases, the best way to get help is to send somebody — or go yourself — to a telephone and make an emergency call by dialling **999**, or by following the instructions for making emergency calls (p. 22). Try to give a clear message — say what has happened and what help you think may be needed.

Send for help

It is always wise to get as much help as you can. In serious injuries, medical help may be necessary. In other conditions, help may be needed to move and lift the casualty. Remember that first-aid can be badly applied — for example, by trying to do too much by yourself and not sending for help soon enough — so try to give good first-aid and summon assistance in plenty of time.

Use the telephone to get help

How to approach a casualty

— remain cool and calm at all times — you will do much more good by keeping calm than be rushing about in an excited manner.
— try to find out what has happened by looking around, by asking by-standers or by asking the casualty.
— quickly check the casualty in case he is not breathing, is bleeding, or unconscious.
Any casualty who cannot speak to you **in sentences** should be treated as unconscious.

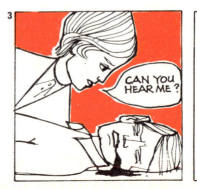

QUICKLY check

1 *Breathing?*
2 *Bleeding?*
3 *Unconscious?*

Apply the correct treatment **at once** if the casualty is **not breathing**, is **bleeding**, or is **unconscious**.

— next, try to find out more about the condition of the casualty.

Ask what happened, what he feels is the matter, whether he has pain anywhere.

Look at, and feel any painful or injured parts.

Compare one arm or leg with the other to see if the injured side is the same shape and size as the good side.

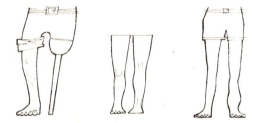

Always compare the good with the injured side

Watch the casualty's face when trying to learn about pain or tenderness.

You will always learn far more by seeing a look of pain on the casualty's face than by asking questions! And if you see a look of pain, you will know that you should be more gentle.

— now, add together all that you know, and decide exactly what is the trouble and what has to be done for the casualty.

— apply the correct treatment.

— send the casualty to hospital or to a doctor. All casualties who appear to have serious injuries or who are obviously ill should be sent to hospital, because doctors are always available there. Extra help and equipment is also readily available in hospital.

A note on gentle handling

It is very important, particularly in the case of a severely injured casualty, to handle him carefully and gently. Rough handling increases pain and worry, and can make injuries considerably worse or bleeding more severe. In good first-aid, there is no place for panic handling. Gentleness is important in all aspects of first-aid, for example, in examining the casualty to find out what is the matter, and in applying splints or slings to fractured limbs.

TWO IMPORTANT RULES IN FIRST-AID

1 The one blanket rule

One blanket is all that is required to cover a casualty who is inside a building, in a sheltered place or in an ambulance.

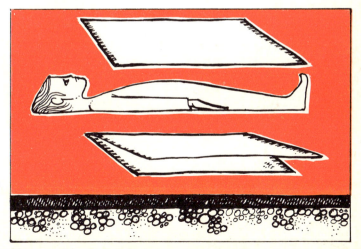

Use one blanket only to cover a casualty

Overheating of all injured people is bad. Hot water bottles should **not** be used in case they give rise to burns, especially if the casualty becomes or is unconscious.

On cold floors, or on the ground, a folded blanket should always be used **under** the casualty. Out of doors, there may be a need for more covering, but the number of blankets should be kept to a minimum.

2 The by mouth rule

Do not give anything to eat or to drink to any casualty, except to conscious burned casualties or to conscious poisoned casualties.

NO Food or Drink for Unconscious casualties

Give nothing by mouth to unconscious casualties

The reasons for this rule are:

i) all **unconscious casualties** and all casualties with **chest and abdominal injuries** should be given NOTHING by mouth because it may choke or further injure them.

ii) many casualties will require an **anaesthetic** shortly after arrival in hospital — and for this it is best to have an empty stomach — so NOTHING should be given by mouth.

iii) **burned casualties** will lose fluid from their body by fluid leaking (a) to form blisters, and (b) through the areas of burned skin — this is often called 'weeping'.

Fluid loss can be a serious problem following burns, and corrective steps should be taken at the earliest possible moment — as a first-aid measure — to deal with the problem of fluid loss.

Conscious adult burned casualties should be given half a cup of water every ten minutes. Children should be given less, according to age (p. 71).

Unconscious burned casualties, like any other unconscious casualty, should be given NOTHING by mouth.

iv) **conscious poisoned casualties** — after the casualty has been made to vomit ('to be sick') he should be given 2 or 3 glasses of water, milk or lemonade, or another normal drink to dilute any remaining poison.

LIFE SAVING FIRST-AID

The correct first-aid treatment for a casualty who is
— not breathing
— bleeding
— unconscious
can save his or her life. So, make sure that you know exactly what to do for each of these conditions.

Life saving first-aid 1

NOT BREATHING

How to recognize that a casualty is not breathing

Look for movement of the chest or movement of the upper part of the abdomen ('stomach') where the ribs separate at the lower end of the breastbone.

Listen with your ear close to the casualty's nose and mouth for breathing. Even if there is a lot of noise you will be able to **feel** his breath in your ear.

Breathing may stop as a result of
head injuries
unconsciousness, from any cause
electrocution
gassing
poisoning
drowning
or other reason

If a person has stopped breathing for four minutes, his life will be in very great danger. His life may be in considerable danger within a shorter time. If he does not breathe for six minutes, he will almost certainly be dead.

Because these emergencies often occur suddenly, and because you will have to act swiftly to be successful, **it is** essential that you know exactly what to do and that **you have practised doing it before the emergency arises.** It is unlikely that you will succeed in saving the casualty's life unless you do the right things in the right order.

The aims of first-aid for not breathing are to

— treat the casualty for blocked breathing.
— give artificial respiration.

If the casualty does not breathe **at once** after treatment for blocked breathing, we must proceed very quickly to the next step, which is to give artificial respiration. Artificial respiration means doing the work of normal breathing for a casualty who is not breathing.

The fact that any casualty is
NOT BREATHING
must be
RECOGNIZED AT ONCE.
There must then be
NO DELAY
in relieving
BLOCKED BREATHING
or in giving
ARTIFICIAL RESPIRATION

---

1   Treat for blocked breathing

The first thing to do for any casualty who is not breathing is to make sure that the casualty has **a clear and unblocked air passage from the nose or mouth to the lungs,** and is not suffering from **blocked breathing.**

Anyone who has stopped breathing will be unconscious. In unconscious people, the tongue may fall backwards and block the back of the throat. **This may be the only reason why an unconscious person cannot breathe.** A conscious person will not suffer in this way because he will move his jaw and tongue to prevent it, but an unconscious person may easily die from blocked breathing.

Blood or vomit may also block the throat of an unconscious person because when he is unconscious, he cannot cough, spit, swallow or move freely.

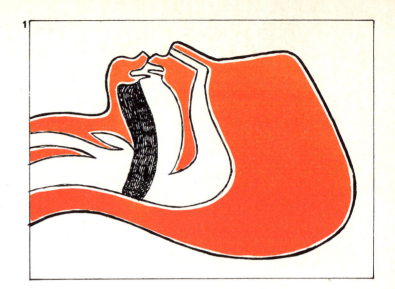

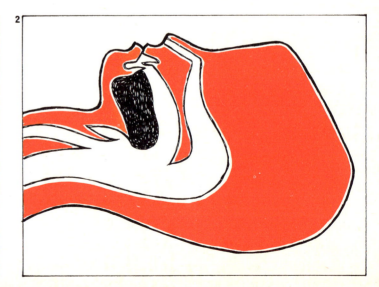

1 *In an unconscious person, the tongue may block the throat*
2 *In a conscious person, the tongue will be kept forward and no blockage will occur*
3 *Bend the head fully back, and the jaw up and forwards to the teeth-clenched position*
4 *In this position, the air passages are clear and unblocked*

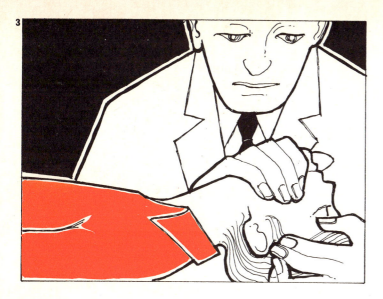

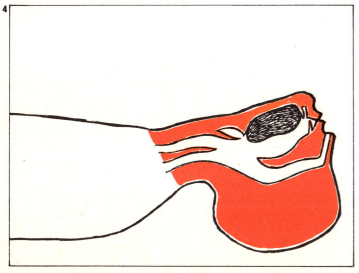

BLOCKED BREATHING is simply remedied

— **first make sure by checking quickly that the mouth is clear of anything which may cause blocking of the air passages,** such as false teeth, loose natural teeth, blood, vomit or debris. Simply clear the mouth with a finger, a handkerchief, or a paper handkerchief, and

— **second, bend the head back firmly as far as it will go and at the same time bring the chin upwards and forwards** until the jaw is fully closed. In this position the front teeth will usually meet. The front of the neck should now make a straight line from the mouth to the top end of the breastbone. Make sure that you bend the head back until it will go no farther. It is surprising to many people how far back the head will go. With the head fully back and the teeth clenched, the tongue cannot fall back and block the throat. If, having quickly cleared the mouth and throat and having bent the neck fully back, the casualty does not **at once** start to breathe, we must proceed to the next step, which is to

2   Give artificial respiration

Artificial respiration should be given by breathing air directly into the casualty's lungs.

HOW TO GIVE ARTIFICIAL RESPIRATION

1   Act immediately

Speed is vital and life depends upon it — the casualty who is not breathing will probably be dead in about four to six minutes. There is, for example, no point in taking a drowning man quickly to land if during this time he could be given artificial respiration in a boat, or if a few breaths of air could be blown into the casualty's lungs in waist-deep water while taking him to dry land. Every second counts: begin artificial respiration at the earliest possible moment.

2   Shift air in and out of the lungs

This is done by breathing (blowing) deeply and slowly through the casualty's nose, while at the same time blocking off the mouth, until the casualty's chest is seen to rise. The rescuer then removes his mouth from the casualty's nose and allows the air to escape from the casualty's lungs. The rescuer should turn his head to watch the chest falling and to avoid the air which escapes from the casualty's lungs. When all the air has escaped, the rescuer should again blow to inflate the casualty's lungs and allow the air to escape. Continue in this manner until the casualty breathes, or for at least an hour.

If for any reason mouth-to-nose artificial respiration cannot be carried out — for example, because the casualty's nose is blocked — then use mouth-to-mouth. One or other of these two methods can always be used, and will succeed in shifting air into the lungs. The first choice is mouth-to-nose, but no time should be lost in changing to blowing through the mouth if mouth-to-nose breathing does not inflate the lungs.

In babies and very young children, after bending the head backwards as far as it will go, the rescuer's mouth should cover **both** the nose and mouth of the baby. Gentle puffs only should be used — just sufficient to cause a good rise of the chest. The first six to ten puffs should be given as rapidly as possible. Blow again, allow all the air to escape, then begin again. The rate should be determined in this way, by the casualty's own needs.

The rescuer's mouth should cover both the nose and mouth of small children and babies

In some cases, the casualty may appear to have his air passages full of froth. You cannot remove all this froth by wiping, so do not waste time trying to remove it. As this froth consists largely of **air** in the form of bubbles, all you have to do to shift air in and out of the lungs is to blow the froth into the lungs. So, blow as usual. In this way you will succeed in shifting air into the casualty's lungs.

3   Continue to apply artificial respiration until the casualty breathes

When the casualty starts to breathe by himself, the breaths will be shallow and weak. The rescuer should

Relieve blocked breathing

1   If possible have the casualty on his back. Tilt his head firmly backwards as far as it will go. Rapidly remove dentures, debris, blood, vomit or loose natural teeth.

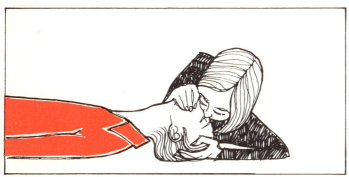

Inflate

2   Breathe deeply and slowly into the casualty's nose, keeping his lips closed with your thumb. If his nose is blocked, breathe through his mouth keeping his nostrils pinched. The chest will rise as it fills with air.

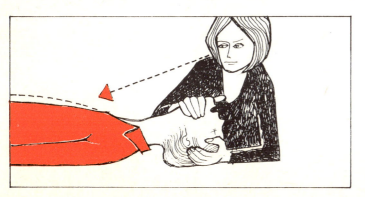

Watch chest falling

3   Take your mouth away and relax. The chest will fall. Inflate again. If the chest does not rise and fall, check his head and neck position as in Fig.1. Continue for at least an hour.

time his inflations to coincide with the casualty's own weak breaths, and should continue to assist the breathing until the casualty appears to be breathing satisfactorily.

Continue to apply artificial respiration to a casualty who is not breathing for not less than an hour or until told by a doctor to stop.

4 Turn the casualty when breathing into the unconscious position

When the casualty is breathing satisfactorily, he will still be unconscious. Following the rules for unconsciousness the casualty should, therefore, be turned into the unconscious position with the head bent back.

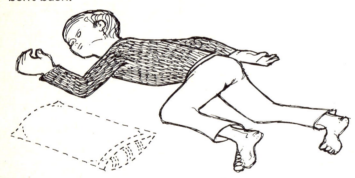

The unconscious position

5 Watch carefully to see that the casualty continues to breathe

Once a casualty has started to breathe there is no guarantee that he will continue to do so. Watch carefully for any sign of weakening of breathing. If you see that breathing is weak, turn the casualty on to his back and

re-commence artificial respiration to assist natural breathing. If breathing stops, turn the casualty on to his back and begin artificial respiration at once.

6 Arrange for the casualty to be taken to hospital

Do not be in too much of a hurry to move the casualty. Although the casualty needs to be in hospital as quickly as possible, make sure that natural breathing is well established before attempting to move him. This will ensure a live casualty arriving at the hospital. Continue to watch carefully during the journey and be prepared to start artificial respiration again at any time. The casualty should, of course, be carried in the unconscious position with the head bent back so that he does not suffer from blocked breathing.

A footnote to not breathing

Be sure that you know how to relieve blocked breathing, and practise artificial respiration **before** any emergency arises. Half-knowing what to do will not save lives. Half-doing these procedures may harm the casualty or may lose a life by preventing somebody else from doing the right things. If you don't know what to do, you cannot save a life; if you do know, and can act, then you may be rewarded by saving the life of a fellow human being. And who knows whose life this may be?

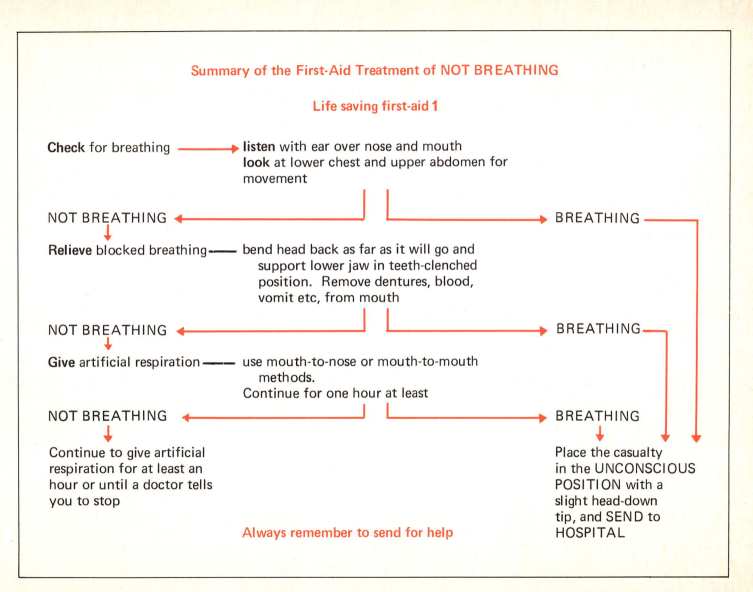

Summary of the First-Aid Treatment of NOT BREATHING

Life saving first-aid 1

Check for breathing ⟶ **listen** with ear over nose and mouth
look at lower chest and upper abdomen for movement

NOT BREATHING ⟵   BREATHING

Relieve blocked breathing — bend head back as far as it will go and support lower jaw in teeth-clenched position. Remove dentures, blood, vomit etc, from mouth

NOT BREATHING ⟵   BREATHING

Give artificial respiration — use mouth-to-nose or mouth-to-mouth methods.
Continue for one hour at least

NOT BREATHING ⟵   BREATHING

Continue to give artificial respiration for at least an hour or until a doctor tells you to stop

Place the casualty in the UNCONSCIOUS POSITION with a slight head-down tip, and SEND to HOSPITAL

Always remember to send for help

Life saving first-aid 2

BLEEDING

The AIMS of FIRST-AID for BLEEDING are to
— stop bleeding quickly.
— send the casualty to hospital without delay.
If blood is lost from the body in other than small amounts, the blood must be replaced by transfusion SOON. This can usually be done only in a hospital.

How to stop bleeding
Bleeding ceases naturally when blood stops **flowing** and forms a **clot**. First-aid treatment should therefore aim to stop blood flowing by
— **pressing** on the place where the blood is coming from
— **elevating limbs**, that is by lifting up arms and legs
— **aiding clot formation by rest**, because movement breaks up blood clot.

If you find a casualty who is bleeding from a wound
1　**Tell him to lie down**
2　**Press firmly over and around the bleeding area or wound.** Use the cleanest thing which is available — a wound dressing if you have one, or a clean handkerchief, towel or other item of clean linen. If nothing else is available in emergency, press with your bare hand and fingers. You can always stop bleeding by pressing on the bleeding spot and by keeping the pressure on.
3　If the bleeding is from an arm or leg, after you have tied a firm dressing in place or while you are still holding the bleeding point with your hand to stop the bleeding, **lift up the arm or leg.** This makes bleeding less severe.

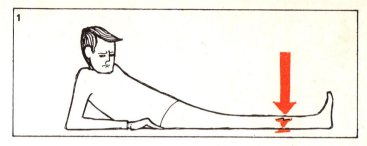
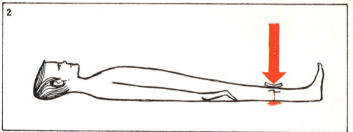
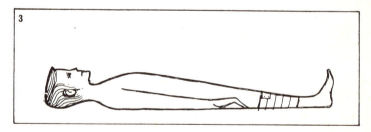
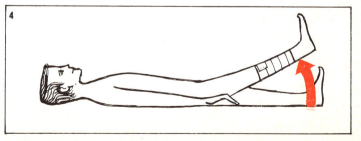

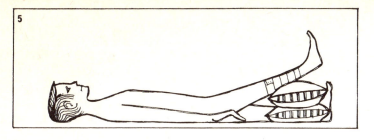

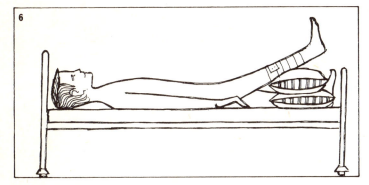

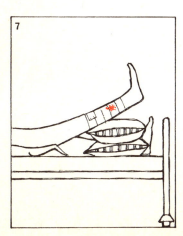

4   If bleeding continues through the dressing which you have applied, **put on another dressing over the one which is already there and tie it on even more firmly.** NEVER remove dressings which are already in place — this disturbs any blood clot and can easily make bleeding worse.

5   Reassure the casualty that bleeding has stopped. A casualty who is worried or agitated will not lie still and will therefore tend to bleed more severely.

6   Send the casualty to hospital soon.

How to stop external bleeding

1   *Press where the blood comes from*
2   *Continue pressing and tell the casualty to lie down*
3   *Bandage a dressing onto the wound*
4   *Elevate*
5   *Keep elevated*
6   *Rest the casualty and send swiftly to hospital if there is much loss of blood*

If bleeding continues

7   *Apply more pressure by putting another dressing on top and bandaging it more firmly*
8   *Elevate higher*

NEVER remove existing dressings

Internal bleeding

A casualty may bleed inside himself — for example, into the chest cavity. This sort of bleeding is called **internal bleeding** and may follow an injury, especially a crush or stab injury, or may result from disease.

Blood may show — for example, if the casualty spits up or vomits blood — or the blood may not show. If the blood does not show, it may be quite difficult to decide if the casualty is, or is not bleeding. If he is bleeding, he will probably **look pale** and may **feel faint or dizzy,** and his pulse rate will gradually become more rapid.

If you think that any casualty is or may be bleeding internally, you should put the casualty at rest by telling him to lie down, and arrange for swift removal to hospital. Casualties who are bleeding internally may require urgent blood transfusion — and must reach hospital quickly.

Bleeding from the nose

The casualty should grasp the nose firmly just below the hard part at the same time keeping the head forward over a basin or bowl. This should be kept up for ten minutes by the clock. After ten minutes, release slowly. No blood will be seen coming from the nose if bleeding has stopped. Tell the casualty not to blow his nose for the next few hours.

If bleeding begins again or has not stopped, repeat the pressure for ten minutes. If bleeding still does not stop, send the casualty to hospital in a sitting position with his head forward over a basin or bowl, still grasping the soft part of the nose.

Pinch the lower soft part of the nose for ten minutes

Wounds

A wound is any break in the skin or other body surface which arises from injury. For example, a cut finger and a cut inside the mouth are both wounds.

The AIMS of FIRST-AID for WOUNDS are to
— stop bleeding (keep blood in).
— prevent infection (keep germs out).

1   Stop bleeding
How to stop bleeding is dealt with above (p. 60).

2   Prevent infection
Everything which comes into contact with a wound should if possible be completely free from germs (sterile). The skin of your hands always has germs on it, so try not to touch a wound even with washed hands. Use sterile dressings. Put the sterile dressing on to the wound without touching the surface of the dressing which will be next to the wound. Once dressings are in place do not take them off again. When wounds have been dressed to stop bleeding and to prevent infection, the first-aid treatment is over except to transport the casualty to hospital quickly.

A word of warning about certain types of wounds
Stab wounds and punctured wounds can cause serious deep injury or can plant infection deep inside the body. These wounds can be caused, for example, by knives (see the warning on p. 16) or knitting needles. Although the skin wound is often small these injuries should always be regarded as serious — especially in the head and neck, around joints and near body cavities such as the chest or abdomen, and in the hand. Do not attempt home treatment in such cases. Apply first-aid treatment and send the casualty to hospital.

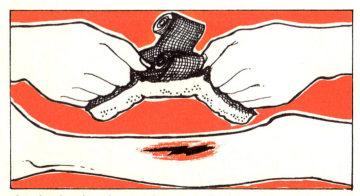

Apply the dressing to the wound without touching the inner sterile surface of the dressing pad

Life Saving First-Aid 2

EXTERNAL BLEEDING   **INTERNAL BLEEDING**

RECOGNIZE that BLEEDING is OCCURRING

STOP the BLEEDING

— PRESS where the blood is coming from
— ELEVATE arm or leg
— REST to aid clot formation and stop clot breaking

BLEEDING CONTINUES   BLEEDING STOPS

— Press more firmly
— ELEVATE higher
— ADD dressings ON TOP
   of existing dressings
   and bandage more
   firmly

This should stop the
bleeding

SEND TO HOSPITAL

if blood loss has been other
than very little, blood
replacement may be needed.
If bleeding has been
moderate or severe, send
quickly to hospital

RECOGNIZE that BLEEDING is OCCURRING
— pale colour, feeble pulse
— blood may be coughed or vomited, etc
   (visible internal bleeding)

REST the casualty,
   tell him to lie down and be still

SEND to HOSPITAL
   quickly if blood loss is due to
   internal bleeding

Always remember to send for help

64

BANDAGING

The aims of bandaging in first-aid are:
— to keep a dressing in place.
— to apply pressure to a dressing or wound.
— to provide support.
— to prevent movement.

How to fold a triangular bandage to make a broad or a narrow bandage

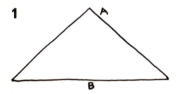

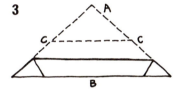

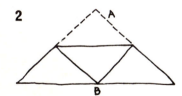

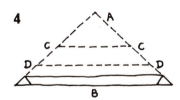

1   Fold A to B
2   Folded
3   Now fold CC to B to make a broad bandage
4   Fold the top of the broad bandage again to B. This makes a narrow bandage

The broad or narrow bandages can be used to hold dressings in place or to tie the legs together.

The end of the bandage should be securely tied in a reef bow. A reef bow has the advantage over a knot that it can be easily untied, thus saving the casualty discomfort when the bandages are removed in hospital.

Tie the bow on the uninjured side, or over an uninjured limb. Make sure that the casualty is not resting on the bow, as this can be very unpleasant. Remember, an unconscious casualty cannot tell you that a bow or knot is pressing into him.

There will be occasions when no triangular bandages are available and improvisations are essential, for example by using scarves, ties, belts, folded handkerchiefs or similar items. Adhesive tape and cellulose tape may be very useful to fix dressings on regions which are difficult to bandage, such as the face.

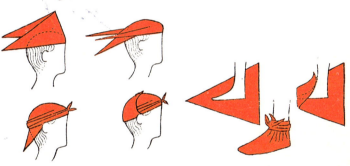

Head bandage   Foot bandage

Roller bandaging

Begin bandaging limbs at the lowest point and work upwards — that is, begin nearest the fingers or toes and bandage towards the shoulder or hip. Start the bandage around the narrow part of a limb. First fix the bandage to the limb by overlapping the first few turns. Then gradually bandage upwards and over the dressing, overlapping each turn of the bandage Finish beyond the dressing by pinning the bandage with a safety-pin, by using adhesive tape, or by tying a reef knot in the split end of the bandage.

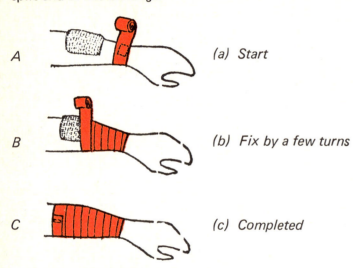

A   (a) Start

B   (b) Fix by a few turns

C   (c) Completed

UNCONSCIOUSNESS

People frequently die following unconsciousness because when they are unconscious they are unable to help themselves and may easily choke, stop breathing and die. Any departure from full normal alertness should be a warning that first-aid may be required. Any person who cannot speak to you **in sentences** (not in words or grunts) should be treated for unconsciousness

The AIMS of FIRST-AID for UNCONSCIOUSNESS are to

— make sure that the casualty can breathe and that he will not suffer from blocked breathing.

— send the casualty to hospital as soon as possible, keeping him in the unconscious position.

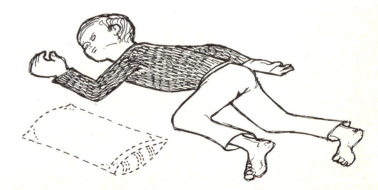

The unconscious position

66

How to treat unconsciousness from any cause

The first aim is to make sure that the casualty can breathe and that he will not suffer from blocked breathing.

1 Relieve blocked breathing (pp. 53-5) by bending the neck fully back and by removing blood, vomit, loose natural teeth, false teeth or debris from the mouth and throat.

2 Place the casualty in the unconscious position with a head-down tip. This will make sure that the casualty can continue to breathe and that any blood, vomit or fluid will run out of the mouth and will not block the back of the throat. It will also make sure that the tongue does not fall back and block the throat.

3 Send the casualty to hospital, keeping him in the unconscious position with a head-down tip.

Any casualty who is breathing and is
— obviously unconscious
  or
— not fully alert
  or
— cannot reply to questions in sentences (not words or grunts)
MUST
— have any blocked breathing relieved
— be placed in the unconscious position, with a slight head-down tip
— be sent to hospital as soon as possible

Unconscious casualties must

— BE GIVEN NOTHING TO EAT OR DRINK in case they choke.
— NEVER BE LEFT ALONE in case they become restless and excited and thus injure themselves further, or
stop breathing and thus require artificial respiration.

All casualties who are or have been unconscious must be
SENT TO HOSPITAL
or
SEEN BY A DOCTOR.

Until you can pass the care of an unconscious person over to an adult or to ambulance attendants or to a doctor, you must stay with the casualty and watch carefully that he does not stop breathing. Unconscious casualties must **never** be left alone.

Some people who have had a 'knock-out' or have recovered from unconsciousness may behave rather peculiarly when they recover consciousness. For example, they may be aggressive and may insist that they do not need to go to hospital or be seen by a doctor. If this happens, point out to them that they are not expert in what to do following recovery from unconsciousness and that what you have said is correct. Try to persuade them to follow your advice — and get other people to back you up in this. If the casualty insists on not following your advice, you cannot stop him from disregarding it!

A word of warning about other injuries in unconscious casualties

Always remember to look very carefully for other injuries — particularly of the head and chest, and for broken limb bones — in unconscious casualties. It is easy to overlook other serious injuries because an unconscious person cannot tell you what has happened or if and where he has pain.

Unconsciousness is a common cause of death which can be prevented by first-aid.

The correct treatment of unconsciousness is probably the way that most lives which **could** be saved by first-aid **would** be saved. For example, many of the people who die on the roads soon after injury have no serious injuries. They die because they become unconscious from a slight head injury and when unconscious they suffer from blocked breathing and die. These deaths are preventable by good first-aid. So, if you ever see anyone who is unconscious, make sure that they can breathe and have no blockage to breathing, and then place them in the unconscious position with a head-down tip if possible. In this simple and effective way you can easily save a life.

Fits (Convulsions)

A fit is unconsciousness plus twitching or violent movements of the limbs and body. Casualties with fits should be placed in the unconscious position, with a head-down tip if possible. If it is necessary to restrain the casualty's movements to prevent further injury, this must be done gently. Movements should not be stopped by force — this will do further harm. Gentle restraint is enough. Move all hard objects such as chairs and tables out of range of the casualty's arms and legs. When the fit is over, send the casualty to hospital in the unconscious position.

Fainting

A faint is a common condition which results in **unconsciousness.** The treatment of fainting is exactly the same as for any other cause of unconsciousness (p. 66).

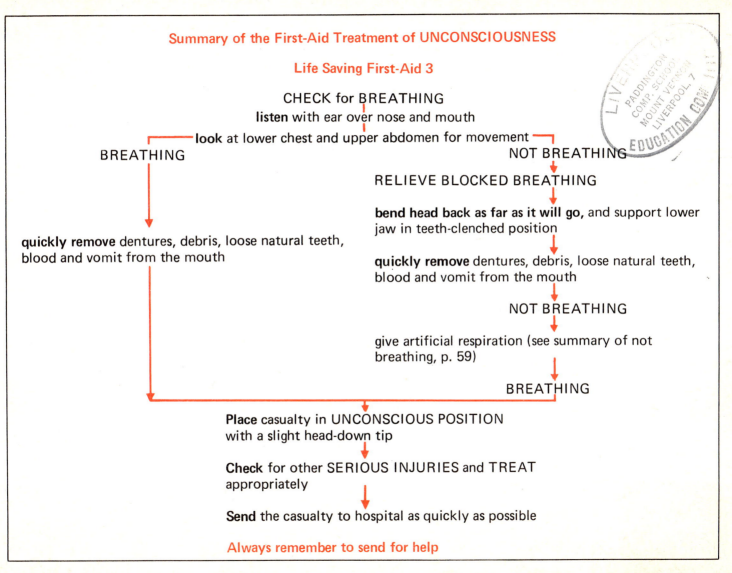

Summary of the First-Aid Treatment of UNCONSCIOUSNESS

Life Saving First-Aid 3

CHECK for BREATHING
listen with ear over nose and mouth
look at lower chest and upper abdomen for movement

BREATHING

NOT BREATHING

RELIEVE BLOCKED BREATHING

bend head back as far as it will go, and support lower jaw in teeth-clenched position

quickly remove dentures, debris, loose natural teeth, blood and vomit from the mouth

quickly remove dentures, debris, loose natural teeth, blood and vomit from the mouth

NOT BREATHING

give artificial respiration (see summary of not breathing, p. 59)

BREATHING

Place casualty in UNCONSCIOUS POSITION with a slight head-down tip

Check for other SERIOUS INJURIES and TREAT appropriately

Send the casualty to hospital as quickly as possible

Always remember to send for help

First-aid to prevent worsening 1

BURNS

Heat burns are injuries caused by heat. A scald is a heat burn produced by a hot liquid. Chemicals can also cause burns by chemical action in the tissues. Most burns are preventable and the majority occur in the home. The bigger a burn is, the more serious it is.

The AIMS of FIRST-AID for BURNS are to

— prevent further damage.
— Prevent germs getting on to the burn.
— replace fluids which will be lost through the burned skin.
— send the casualty to hospital.

Heat burns

Immediate cooling of heat burns and scald both lessens the severity of the injury and relieves pain.

ALL HEAT BURNS AND SCALDS SHOULD BE COOLED AS QUICKLY AS POSSIBLE AFTER THE INJURY.

The easiest way to do this is to get the casualty under a cool shower or into a bath, or to put the burned part under a running tap of cold water or into a basinful of cold water. Clothing should be removed after cooling has begun unless it is stuck. Stuck clothing should be left.

COOLING SHOULD BE CONTINUED FOR TEN MINUTES, TIMED BY THE CLOCK.

During this time, send for an ambulance but do not move the casualty until ten minutes has been spent on cooling the burn or scald. If it is not possible to cool the burn on the spot, the casualty should go immediately or be taken by the first available suitable transport to where cooling can be carried out.

Next, **cover the burn** with a large dressing — sterile if possible. If there is not a sterile dressing to hand, use the cleanest **non-fluffy** covering which is available. At home freshly laundered linen such as pillow cases can be used. Make sure that the dressing is large enough to cover an area **bigger** than the burn. If the burn is large, use several dressings.

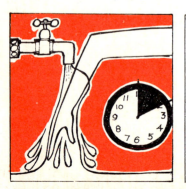

Cool burns and scalds at once and continue cooling for ten minutes

Cover the burn with the cleanest non-fluffy cover available

DO NOT apply lotions, antiseptics or anything greasy to the burn.

DO NOT use hairy lint or fluffy material to cover a burn.

People who have burns which are larger than the size of the palm of their hand should be sent quickly to hospital as soon as the burn has been covered. The casualty, **if conscious**, should be given sips of water every ten minutes until he reaches hospital.

Give sips (not gulps) of water every ten minutes until the burned person reaches hospital

Every ten minutes give

adults	½cup
children of 11 years and over	⅓ cup
children of 5 years and over	¼ cup
children under 5 years should be given only small sips	

More than these quantities may cause vomiting — so give the correct amount. Remember that unconscious casualties should be given **nothing** by mouth.

Scalds

After cooling, treat as a heat burn.

Chemical burns are burns by acids, alkalis or similar liquids.

Remove the chemical from the eyes and the skin by washing AT ONCE, with **large amounts** of running water. The eyes should be washed out **first** as chemicals can very easily damage the eyes. Hold the eyelids apart to make sure that the water can wash out the chemical. Remove all clothes which may have any chemical on them. Continue washing with large amounts of water — preferably from a tap, shower, hose or spray — for **TEN** minutes, timed by the clock. Do not skimp or hurry this step as the chemical will go on burning if it has not been properly washed off.

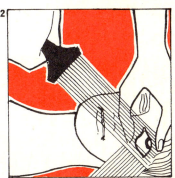

Chemical in the eye
Use large amounts of water and flush for ten minutes
1   Self-help
2 & 3 First-help
Hold the eyelids apart

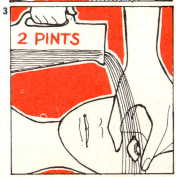

2 PINTS

Electrical burns

Make sure that the electricity is switched off before approaching the casualty. If you are not **sure** that the current is off, DO NOT touch the casualty in case **you** are electrocuted. Do not touch or go into any water or other liquid in which the casualty is lying as the liquid can conduct electricity. Shout for help.

When the electricity is off and you can safely approach the casualty, listen immediately to check whether he is breathing or not. If he is not breathing, begin artificial respiration at once (see pp. 56-8) and continue until the casualty breathes, or for at least an hour. Turn the casualty into the unconscious position after breathing begins. Then, treat any serious burns as a heat burn, and send the casualty quickly to hospital.

Cold water as first-aid for burns

In heat burns, showering for ten minutes will **cool** the burn; in chemical burns, showering for ten minutes, with prior and special attention to the eyes, will **remove** and **dilute** the chemical. In both cases further damage will be minimized.

Summary of first-aid of BURNS

Heat burns and scalds

1 Cool immediately ⟶ put the casualty into a cool shower or bath, or put the burned part under a running tap of cold water or in a basinful of cold water

2 Continue cooling for 10 minutes ⟶ do not skimp or hurry this step

3 Cover the burned areas and adjacent skin ⟶ use a sterile dressing, if possible, or the cleanest, **non-fluffy** cover available

4 Replace fluids ⟶ if the casualty is conscious, give sips of water every 10 minutes (see p. 71 for quantities). Give nothing by mouth to unconscious casualties

5 Send to hospital ⟶ continue to give **sips** of water every 10 minutes

Chemical burns

1 Remove the chemical AT ONCE ⟶ wash **at once** with large amounts of running water from a tap, shower, hose or spray. Remove clothing which may have chemical on it. **Give prior and special attention to the eyes,** holding the lids apart to let water in

2 Continue flushing with water for 10 minutes ⟶ do not skimp or hurry this step. The chemical must be adequately removed

3 Continue as indicated under heat burns, 3

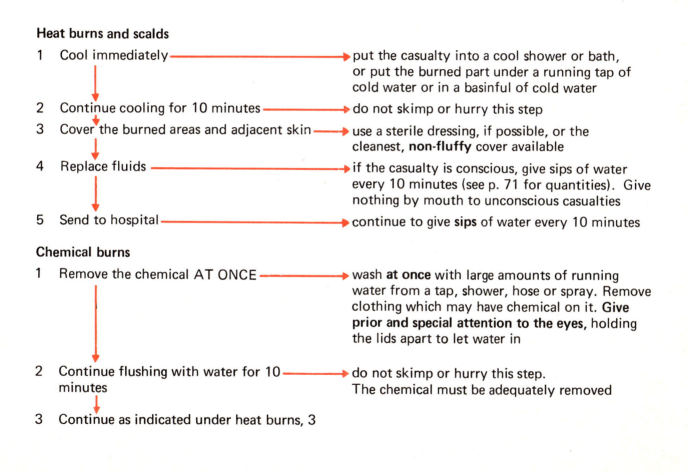

Electrical burns

1   Make sure that the ELECTRICITY is ———▶ do not become the next casualty yourself
    OFF before going near the casualty

2   When the electricity is off, approach
    and LISTEN for BREATHING

    breathing   not breathing ————▶ if breathing has stopped, give artificial
                                            respiration (pp. 56-8)

3   Check for unconsciousness

    conscious   unconscious ————▶ if unconscious, place in the unconscious
                                          position

4   If more than half an hour has passed
    since burning, if breathing has been
    stopped, or if the casualty has been
    or is unconscious ————————————————▶ omit cooling, cover all burns, send quickly
                                          to hospital

5   If none of 1-4 above apply, continue
    as indicated under heat burns, 1.

Always remember to send for help

First-aid to prevent worsening 2

FRACTURES AND DISLOCATIONS

1 Fractures

A fracture is a broken or cracked bone.

A **closed** fracture has no wound at or near it. The skin is not broken, although it may be bruised and swollen.

An **open** fracture is a fracture plus a wound at or near the fracture.

How to tell if there is a fracture

When any part of the body has had a heavy blow or twist, and the part is

painful

tender to touch

mis-shapen or swollen, and

the casualty cannot use the part normally

then it can safely be assumed that

the bone is broken.

An X-ray picture taken in hospital may be the only sure way of knowing that a bone is broken. If there is any doubt about whether a bone is or is not broken, always treat the casualty as if the bone is broken. In this way, you will always do the right thing and will never do harm.

The AIMS of FIRST-AID for FRACTURES are to

— cover all **open** fractures.

— keep the fractured parts still.

Cover all open fractures

Because an open fracture is a fracture plus a wound, we should first treat the wound in order to stop bleeding and to keep germs out. When bleeding has been stopped and the wound has been covered, the treatment of open and closed fractures is the same.

Keep the fractured parts still

Prevent further damage and pain **by stopping movement from occurring at or near the ends of the broken bone.**

In order to stop movement taking place at a break in the bone, it is usually necessary to prevent any movement for some distance above and below the region of the break. For example, if there is a fracture of the leg below the knee, it is necessary to stop movement occurring from just below the hip above the fracture, to beyond the ankle below. The process of stopping movement from occurring around the broken bone is called 'immobilizing the fracture' and is a very important part of the treatment. When the fracture or suspected fracture has been immobilized, send the casualty to hospital.

Fractures of the upper limb

In the upper limbs, the best way to stop movement from occurring at a break in the bone is to put on an arm sling.

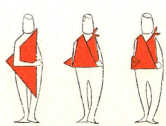

Arm sling

Improvised slings

1 *Arm inside coat*
2 *Coat flap turned up and pinned*
3 *Belt supporting arm*

Send the casualty to hospital in the first available transport sitting up, as this position is usually the most comfortable.

If the break is near the elbow, do not try to bend the elbow in order to apply an arm sling. In this case tell the casualty to lie down, and place the arm gently on a pillow. Another method of keeping the arm still is to put some padding between the arm and the side of the body, and gently move the injured arm in to the side on to the padding. Then tie the arm loosely to the trunk.

Always tie above and below the site of a break, NEVER over the break.

A fractured elbow — lay the injured arm palm up on pillows

Fracture of the lower limb

In the lower limbs, the best way to stop movement from occurring at a break in the bone is to tie the good leg to the injured one.

Transport the casualty to hospital lying down.

Ankle and leg

If the break is near the ankle, place one or two pillows, cushions or rolled-up coats or jackets under the leg. Tie these loosely on to the leg to stop the leg rolling off or moving.

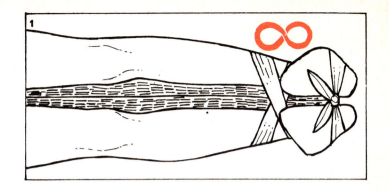

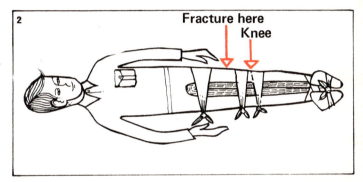

Fracture here
Knee

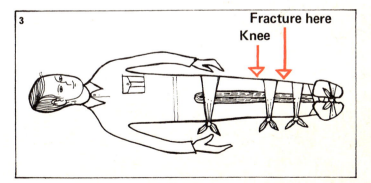

Fracture here
Knee

1 *Tie the feet and ankles with a figure-of-eight bandage*
2 *Tie above and below the break and send for help*
3 *Tie above and below the break and send for help*

Thigh, hip and pelvis

If there is a break in the thigh bone, the hip or pelvis, the casualty has to be kept still from the armpits to the feet in order to stop movement. Tie the feet and legs together and transport to hospital lying down on a stretcher

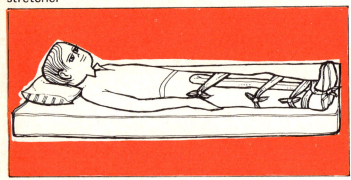

First-aid for a fractured pelvis or thigh

Fracture of the spine

A broken neck or back is a very serious injury and should only be treated by a doctor or an experienced adult first-aider. The casualty will probably complain of pain in the neck or back, and will usually have had a fall or will have been in a road accident.

If you think a casualty has fractured his spine, you should tell the casualty to lie still, and tell other people not to move him. Send for a doctor and an ambulance at once telling them that you think the casualty has a fractured spine. Until this help arrives, **see that the casualty does not move and make sure that no one else tries to move him or her.** With a broken neck or back, serious permanent damage can easily result to the spinal cord if the casualty is moved carelessly — and this may

result in permanent loss of use of the legs (paralysis) together with total numbness. This is why if you suspect a fractured spine, you must make sure that you do not allow any further harm to come to the casualty by movement.

SUMMARY of first-aid for FRACTURES

RECOGNIZE that the bone may be broken
- how did the injury happen? eg, twisted, struck, fall, etc
- pain
- tenderness
- mis-shapen or swollen
- the part cannot be used normally

CHECK for WOUNDS at or near the fracture, and treat

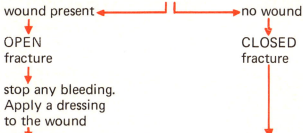

wound present ← → no wound

OPEN fracture

CLOSED fracture

stop any bleeding.
Apply a dressing
to the wound

PREVENT MOVEMENT at or near the site of the break

Tell the casualty to KEEP STILL.

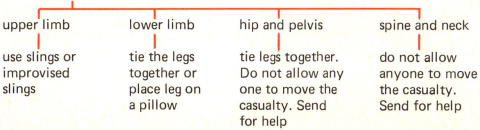

upper limb	lower limb	hip and pelvis	spine and neck
use slings or improvised slings	tie the legs together or place leg on a pillow	tie legs together. Do not allow any one to move the casualty. Send for help	do not allow anyone to move the casualty. Send for help

SEND to HOSPITAL for X-rays and further treatment

Always remember to send for help

2 Dislocations

A dislocation is present when a bone has been displaced at a joint from its normal position. Pain, tenderness, swelling and lack of use of the limb will be present when a joint is dislocated. The part may be mis-shapen. Fractures and dislocations often occur together and therefore an X-ray will be needed in injuries around a joint to decide whether the injury is a fracture, a dislocation, or both.

The treatment of a dislocation is similar to that of a fracture — immobilize the injured joint. NEVER try to put a dislocation right — this is a job for a doctor. Prevent movement from occurring and send the casualty to hospital.

First-aid to prevent worsening 3

HEAD INJURIES

Injuries to the head can be serious — so, anyone who has had a bang or blow on the head and who does not remember what happened, who was 'knocked out' or unconscious even for a few seconds, MUST be sent to hospital or be seen by a doctor. Unconscious casualties should be treated for unconsciousness (pp. 66-9).

If the casualty has recovered consciousness, keep him quiet and relaxed by asking him to lie down in a comfortable position. If the casualty again becomes dreamy or unconscious, he must be placed in the unconscious position and sent **quickly** to hospital. Any false teeth, loose natural teeth, blood, vomit or debris should be removed from the mouth. Watch breathing carefully until the casualty arrives at

hospital to make sure that he does not stop breathing (p. 67).

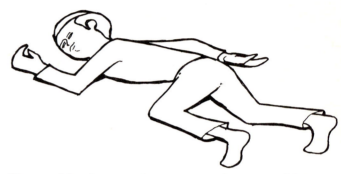

NO Food or Drink for Unconscious casualties

Give nothing by mouth to unconscious casualties

Wounds of the head should be treated in the same way as other wounds — by applying a dressing to the wound to stop bleeding and to keep germs out — except that in head injuries you should not press hard on the wound in case there is a fracture of the skull underneath. If you press too hard, you may push a piece of bone into the brain. Gentle pressure **around the edges** of a scalp wound will always stop bleeding, and will do no damage to the brain.

Black eye

All black eyes MUST be seen by a doctor, to exclude serious eye injury or a fracture of the skull. Therefore, any casualty who has a black eye must be sent to hospital or to a doctor.

First-aid for POISONING by MOUTH

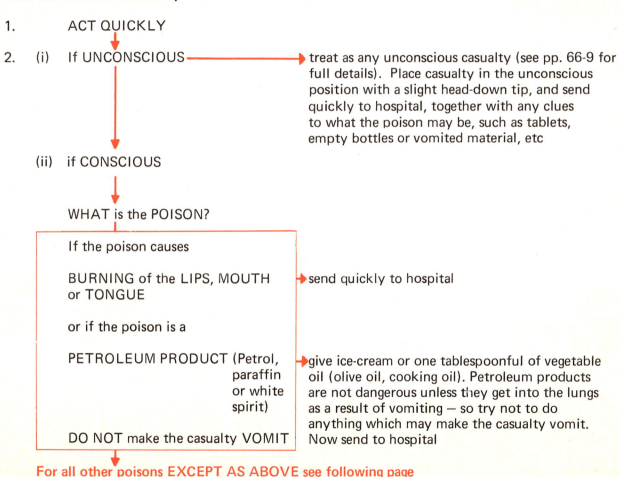

1.   ACT QUICKLY

2.   (i)   If UNCONSCIOUS ⟶ treat as any unconscious casualty (see pp. 66-9 for full details). Place casualty in the unconscious position with a slight head-down tip, and send quickly to hospital, together with any clues to what the poison may be, such as tablets, empty bottles or vomited material, etc

     (ii)   if CONSCIOUS

           WHAT is the POISON?

           If the poison causes

           BURNING of the LIPS, MOUTH or TONGUE ⟶ send quickly to hospital

           or if the poison is a

           PETROLEUM PRODUCT (Petrol, paraffin or white spirit) ⟶ give ice-cream or one tablespoonful of vegetable oil (olive oil, cooking oil). Petroleum products are not dangerous unless they get into the lungs as a result of vomiting — so try not to do anything which may make the casualty vomit. Now send to hospital

           DO NOT make the casualty VOMIT

For all other poisons EXCEPT AS ABOVE see following page

For ALL OTHER POISONS

EXCEPT THOSE IN THE BOX ON PAGE 81

MAKE the casualty VOMIT by giving → 2 tablespoonsful of salt in a glass of warm water
OR
2 teaspoonsful of mustard in a glass of warm water
OR
put a finger down his throat (his finger or yours) to depress the tongue and touch the back of the throat

DILUTE any remaining poison → give two or three glasses of water, (or milk or lemonade, etc)

then, SEND QUICKLY TO HOSPITAL

ALWAYS SEND CLUES to HOSPITAL → send empty bottles, tablets, vomited material, berries or anything else which you think may help the doctors in hospital to identify the poison and the dose

Always remember to send for help

WET-COLD CHILLING (wet-cold exposure)

Every year some hill-walkers, climbers and hikers get into trouble in hilly or mountainous country due to wet-cold chilling. Most of this trouble is due to lack of proper clothing and equipment and to lack of awareness of the dangers of wet-cold. Even in summer, conditions in hilly or mountainous country can change quickly from fine to very wet and cold. Anyone who is ill-prepared for these conditions can easily die from wet-cold chilling. Loss of body heat occurs in quite a short time, particularly if the person is tired or exhausted, and death may occur quite quickly as a result of chilling.

How to prevent wet-cold chilling

Equipment

Waterproof clothing and overgarments would prevent most wet-cold chilling casualties

Plasticized nylon trousers, anoraks, macintoshes and capes are cheap and easily obtainable. If these are worn over ordinary windproof clothing, wetness should not be able to penetrate inwards.

It is a good idea to have a large light-weight waterproof cape in which you can bivouac — that is, make a little tent and sit down and rest, so that if conditions become adverse, rest and shelter are possible.

A **torch and a whistle** should be carried to attract attention in case of collapse, injury or other trouble.

Spare clothing, including trousers and gloves should be carried **in a waterproof plastic bag** in the rucksack. Bright orange-red is the best colour in most places.

Clothing to prevent wet-cold chilling

See what the experts wear, and copy them. Stout shoes or boots should be worn on hill walks — sandals and plimsolls are quite unsuitable.

Leadership

No party of young people should venture out in wild, open or mountainous country without trained and experienced adult leaders. Never go alone.

Shelter

If the weather worsens, or any member of a party shows any likelihood of becoming wet or tired, shelter should be sought AT ONCE. It is foolish to wait until exhaustion and collapse occur before seeking shelter.

Camping is the surest way of preventing disaster when a person shows any sign of wet-cold chilling, provided that members of the party can remain warm and dry in camp.

Obtain a weather forecast before setting out

Forecasting services exist which can be contacted by telephone. Before setting out, it is wise to obtain a **detailed and up-to-date** forecast from the nearest weather forecasting station — see the telephone directory for details.

Inform others of the intended route

Always inform some responsible person of the intended route and the expected time of arrival at the destination. Such information is vital should rescue become necessary. Any would-be rescuer must make sure that he does not himself become a casualty through being inadequately trained, prepared, or equipped.

Fitness

Reasonable fitness is essential. Never set out on an expedition of any kind if you feel even slightly unwell. You may endanger others as well as yourself if you collapse or cannot continue walking in wild, open or mountainous country. If you feel unwell at any time after starting, tell the leader of the party **at once.**

How to recognize wet-cold chilling

in the early stages
— be aware that wet-cold chilling may occur.
— look out for any person who becomes dreamy and slow in his responses, or tired, listless and not-caring. Any departure from normal behaviour should be viewed with suspicion.
— weakness, slowing, excessive tiredness, stumbling and repeated falling appear — probably in that order.

in the late stages
— collapse, and unconsciousness occur.
— cramp, loss of feeling in the legs, loss of movement and fits may occur in some cases.

How to treat wet-cold chilling

Casualties who suffer from wet-cold chilling should be **dried** and **heated.** This is the **only** exception to the rule that a casualty must not be warmed.
— prevent further heat loss by removing wet clothing and by drying the casualty with warm towels if possible.
— put on warm, dry clothing.

- place the casualty in blankets or in the special sleeping bags provided by mountain rescue posts or in a large polythene sack (a suitable polythene sack to carry is one which is 7ft x 4ft 500 gauge).
- give the casualty hot sugared drinks if he is conscious.
- it is much better to dry the casualty, and to place him in warm, dry clothing and blankets **in the first available place** or shelter than to transport him wet for a longer distance — say to a hospital — before making efforts to deal with the condition. **Because the illness is caused by chilling and loss of body heat, the sooner this process can be reversed, the better are the chances of a favourable outcome.**
- if a hot bath can be given to restore body heat, it should be used.
  Failing this, if a sink or basin is available the hands and forearms should be immersed in comfortably hot water to transfer heat.
- during stretcher transport, try to maintain a slight head-down tip.

Home treatment

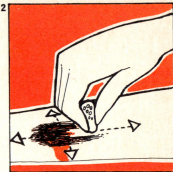

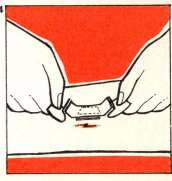

1 First, wash your hands
2 Next, clean the skin around the wound
3 Then clean the wound
4 Apply a dressing

Wounds and cuts

Some minor wounds, cuts and grazes can be treated at home. If you have any doubt at all about whether a wound is minor or serious, apply first-aid treatment (pp. 86-7) and send the casualty to hospital or to a doctor.

The AIMS of HOME TREATMENT for MINOR WOUNDS, CUTS and GRAZES are to
— stop bleeding.
— clean the surrounding skin and the wound.
— apply a suitable dressing.
1 **How to stop bleeding** is dealt with on pp. 60-2
2 **Clean the surrounding skin and the wound**

It is often a good idea to let the injured person clean his own wound. In this way he can decide how much discomfort he can bear, and whether to do things quickly or slowly. As long as a good job is done of the cleaning, it does not matter whether cleaning takes five minutes or forty minutes.

Always begin by washing your hands thoroughly before cleaning a wound. The nails should be scrubbed clean too. If you are going to allow a casualty to clean his own wound, the casualty should wash his or her hands thoroughly too, before beginning.

Cleaning the wound and the surrounding skin

thoroughly is the most important step in getting good wound healing. Dirty wounds heal badly, clean wounds heal well. Therefore, all dirt, grit, hair, loose skin, germs and so on must, as far as possible, be washed off the surrounding skin and out of the wound. Soap and water and a soft long-haired nail brush will usually do very well for this purpose. Take plenty of time and lots of water. Running water is best, but several basinsful will suffice. It is important not only to clean the wound but also to clean the surrounding skin, because any germs there can easily find their way into the wound. Begin by cleaning the surrounding skin and try not to let any dirt from here trickle into the wound. Wipe **away** from the wound edges. When the skin is clean, begin to cleanse the wound. Do not skimp or hurry the wound cleaning: do a good job.

3 Apply a dressing to the wound

The best dressing for a small wound is usually a dry **sterile** unmedicated dressing with sticking plaster — a 'sticky patch'. If the wound is larger than can be covered by a sticky patch, then you should not be treating it by yourself. Apply the patch without touching the sterile dressing or the wound.

A word about antiseptics, ointments and medicated wound dressings

For home use in minor wounds we would recommend:
  For cleansing the wound
  soap and water or Savlon
  For dressing the wound
  sterilized dry unmedicated sticky patches (for example, 'Band-aid')

We do **not** believe in using medicated dressings and ointments on fresh wounds, and think that it is unwise to use any of these as a substitute for thorough wound cleaning followed by a sterile dry dressing. There is nothing to be gained and much to be lost by applying dressings, antiseptics and ointments on top of dirty and germ-infected wounds. The effect of such 'treatment' is to seal the dirt and germs into the wound. Part of nature's defences is to shed dirt, dead skin and germs to the surface of a wound: nothing should therefore be done which will interfere with this process.

Do not use cotton wool or hairy lint when cleansing a wound or for covering a wound or burn. Stray fragments get left behind.

Splinters under the nail or in the finger

If the splinter can be easily grasped by tweezers, it should be removed. Next, the skin surrounding the entrance wound should be thoroughly cleansed as described above. If the splinter has penetrated for a distance of more than this   / (4 mm), the wound should be seen by an adult or a doctor. Splinter wounds can drive dirt and infection in, and are therefore considerably more dangerous than surface wounds of a much larger area.

If the splinter cannot easily be grasped by tweezers and pulled out, send the casualty to an adult or to a doctor.

Burns

Small burns — that is, burns which are no larger in area than this circle ◯ (10 mms diameter) can be treated at home except if the burns are deep or on the face or hands. Clean the burned area and the surrounding skin as described above under wounds, and then apply a sterile dressing.

Sand or grit in the eye

Do not rub the eye.

Tell the casualty to blink rapidly and to look up and down. This may, by movement and as a result of increased tear flow, allow the sand or grit to be dislodged.

If this does not work, tell the casualty to pull the edge of the upper lid over the lower lid by pulling on the upper eyelashes. This may remove the sand or grit.

If the sand or grit is still in the eye, send the casualty to an adult or to a doctor.

APPENDICES

A note for teachers

A note for teachers

Further reading

Useful addresses for further reading

Teaching aids

Index

Notes

Posters, leaflets, publicity material, handouts, notes for teachers, training manuals and guides on all aspects of safty and accident prevention are available from RoSPA (p. 91).

The lists of books for further reading and of useful addresses for further information will provide readily available facts or guidance on most aspects of safety and first-aid to a more advanced level than in this book.

Teaching First-Aid — a book for teachers
Baillière, Tindall & Cassell Ltd, 1970.

Further reading

Further reading

1 **New Essential First Aid**
by A. Ward Gardner and Peter J. Roylance
Pan, London.

2 **The Handbook of First Aid**
by A. Ward Gardner and Peter J. Roylance
Arthur Barker, London.

3 **New Advanced First Aid**
by A. Ward Gardner with Peter J. Roylance
Butterworths, London.

4 **Illustrated Handbook of Life Saving Instruction**
The Royal Life Saving Society, London.

5 **The Highway Code**
HMSO, London.

6 **The New Traffic Signs**
HMSO, London.

7 **The Human Body**
by C. Bibby and I.T. Morrison
Penguin, London.

8 **Fire Prevention Code for the Home**
RoSPA and the Fire Protection Association, London.

9 **Water Safety Code**
RoSPA or HMSO, London.

10 **Safety Afloat**
RoSPA or HMSO, London.

11 **Learn to Swim** (official Amateur Swimming Association leaflet) *published by Bovril Limited, 148 Old Street, London E.C.1.* (on a non-profit basis). Also available in wall chart form which covers swimming strokes, diving, swimming training and survival swimming.

Useful addresses for further reading

Teaching aids

The Royal Society for the Prevention of Accidents,
(RoSPA)
Terminal House,
52 Grosvenor Gardens,
London S.W.1.

The Fire Protection Association,
Aldermary House,
Queen Street,
London E.C.4.

The Royal Life Saving Society,
Desborough House,
14 Devonshire Street,
Portland Place,
London W.1.

Problems
The authors would always be glad to try to help in any
case where a problem could not be solved either by
using the books for further reading or by writing
to the addresses above.

Colour filmstrips (35 mm) and colour filmloops (8 mm)
on the subjects covered in NEW SAFETY AND
FIRST-AID are available from:

Camera Talks Ltd,
31 North Row,
London, W1R 2EN

Telephone 01 - 493 2761

Index

Notes